GALILEO GALILEI
1564–1642 •
Discovered law of pendulum motion

CAROLUS LINNAEUS
• 1707–1778
Classified the plant
and animal kingdoms

SIGMUND FREUD
• 1856–1939
Started psychoanalysis

GREGOR JOHANN MENDEL
1822–1884 •
Discovered principles of heredity

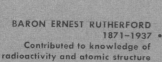

BARON ERNEST RUTHERFORD
1871–1937 •
Contributed to knowledge of
radioactivity and atomic structure

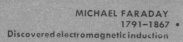

GUGLIELMO MARCONI
• 1874–1937
Invented the wireless telegraph

LOUIS AGASSIZ
• 1807–1873
Investigated glacial motion
and marine life

MICHAEL FARADAY
1791–1867 •
Discovered electromagnetic induction

SIR ISAAC NEWTON
• 1642–1727
Discovered laws of light,
gravity, motion and color

ALBERT EINSTEIN
1879–1955 •
Conceived the Theory of Relativity

WILHELM KONRAD ROENTGEN
• 1845–1923
Discovered X-rays

ALEXANDER GRAHAM BELL
1847–1922 •
Invented
the telephone

JOSEPH LISTER
• 1827–1912
Started antiseptic surgery

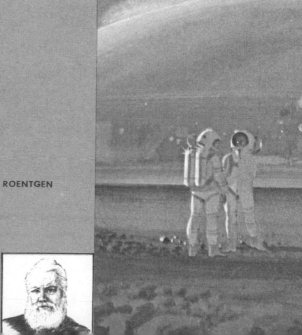

YOUNG PEOPLE'S
SCIENCE
ENCYCLOPEDIA

Edited by the Staff of
NATIONAL COLLEGE OF EDUCATION, Evanston, Ill.

ASSOCIATE EDITORS

HELEN J. CHALLAND, B.E., M.A., PH.D.
Chairman, Science Department, National
College of Education

DONALD A. BOYER, B.S., M.S., PH.D.
Science Education Consultant, Winnetka
Public Schools, Winnetka, Ill., Science,
National College of Education

W. RAY RUCKER, B.A., M.A., ED.D.
Former Dean of the College, National College of Education

EDITORIAL CONSULTANTS
ON THE STAFF OF NATIONAL COLLEGE OF EDUCATION

Elizabeth R. Brandt, B.A., M.Ed.

Eugene B. Cantelupe, B.A., M.F.A., Ph.D.

John H. Daugherty, B.S., M.A.

Irwin K. Feinstein, B.S., M.A., Ph.D.

Mary Gallagher, A.B., M.A., Ph.D.

Beatrice B. Garber, A.B., M.S., Ph.D.

Robert R. Kidder, A.B., M.A., Ph.D.

Jean C. Kraft, B.S., M.A., Ph.D.

Elise P. Lerman, B.A., B.F.A., M.F.A.

Mary-Louise Neumann, A.B., B.S. in L.S.

Lavon Rasco, B.A., M.A., Ph.D.

SPECIAL SUBJECT AREA CONSULTANTS

Krafft A. Ehricke, B.A.E., H.L.D.

Charles B. Johnson, B.S., M.A., M.S.

Raymond J. Johnson, B.B.A., Senior
 Certificate in Industrial Engineering

Norma R. Rucker, B.S.

H. Kenneth Scatliff, M.D.

Ray C. Soliday, B.A., B.S., M.A.
 (Deceased)

Fred R. Wilkin, Jr., B.S., M.Ed.

THE STAFF

PROJECT DIRECTOR	·	WALLACE B. BLACK
COORDINATING EDITOR	·	JEAN F. BLASHFIELD
ART DIRECTOR	·	BEN ROSEN
PHOTO AND ART EDITOR	·	MARTHA O'ROURKE
PRODUCTION EDITOR	·	ORLANDO T. CURCIO

YOUNG PEOPLE'S
SCIENCE
ENCYCLOPEDIA

Edited by the Staff of

NATIONAL COLLEGE OF EDUCATION
Evanston, Illinois

VOLUME 18
SU-VE

 CHILDRENS PRESS, CHICAGO

Revised Edition 1966
© Copyright 1964, U. S. A.
by CHILDRENS PRESS, INC.

All rights reserved
Printed in the United States of America
Library of Congress Catalogue Card Number 61-17925

10 11 12 13 14 15 16 17 18 19 20 21 22 23 24 25   R   70 69

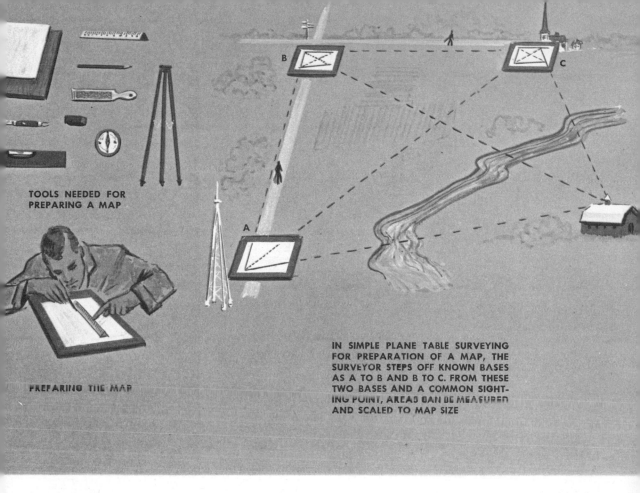

TOOLS NEEDED FOR PREPARING A MAP

PREPARING THE MAP

IN SIMPLE PLANE TABLE SURVEYING FOR PREPARATION OF A MAP, THE SURVEYOR STEPS OFF KNOWN BASES AS A TO B AND B TO C. FROM THESE TWO BASES AND A COMMON SIGHT-ING POINT, AREAS CAN BE MEASURED AND SCALED TO MAP SIZE

Surveying The purpose of surveying is to measure and locate angles, lines, and elevations on the surface of the earth. Principles of geometry and trigonometry are applied to the surveyor's measurements. Distances, boundaries, volumes, areas, and location of points can then be determined. Surveying is used to make maps, to lay out routes for highways, to plan bridges and large buildings, and to define boundaries of land property, counties, states, and countries.

For most surveying purposes, the earth is treated as if it were a plane surface instead of spheroid in shape. In relatively small areas the curvature of the earth does not produce significant errors in measurements. But for large maps of countries, coastlines and the world, *geodetic surveys* are used instead of plane surveys. Geodetic surveys take into account the curvature of the earth.

For land, route, and engineering surveys, the essential tools of the surveyor are the *transit, measuring tapes, levels,* and *compass.*

He also uses *chaining pins* to mark the end location of his tape, a *range pole* painted with red and white bands so it can be used as a sighting rod, and a *plumb bob* in areas of varying elevation. The *transit* is the basic instrument of surveying. It is a small but fine-quality telescope which is on a swiveling frame so that it can be rotated horizontally and vertically. Usually mounted on a tripod, the transit is used to measure distances by using stadia (special rods) instead of tapes, and for measuring horizontal and vertical angles necessary in surveying rough terrain.

Steel tapes varying from 50 to 100 feet in length are used to measure distances. Small variations and errors can be caused by expansion, contraction, or sag of the tape. If particularly precise measurements are required, an *invar* steel tape, made of a nickel-steel alloy, is used because it does not react much to temperature change. If only rough measurements are needed, the surveyor may pace off the distance. The need for precision varies with the purpose of the survey. Construction may call for very precise figures.

In surveys of large areas, *aerial* and *photogrammetric* methods are used along with on-the-ground survey. Airplanes and photographs

1707

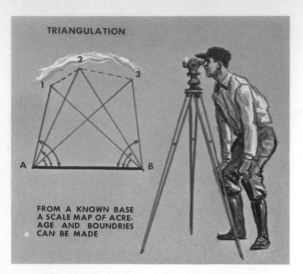

TRIANGULATION

FROM A KNOWN BASE A SCALE MAP OF ACRE- AGE AND BOUNDRIES CAN BE MADE

Nesting holes of cliff swallows in steep cliffs of loess along the Mississippi River

also supplement the ground methods employed in topographical surveying, which produces maps showing elevations and depressions and the contours of the earth's surface.   C. L. K.

SEE ALSO: EARTH, GEOMETRY, MAP-MAKING, MEASUREMENT, PROJECTION

Suspension   see Colloidal state

Suspension bridge   see Bridges

Suture (SOO-tchuhr) A suture is a line resulting from the union, during growth, of two parts, such as two flat bones of the skull. In surgery, it is the line formed by sewing together two pieces of separated tissue.

Swallow Swallows are common birds in the United States. They are all about five or six inches long and have long, narrow, triangular wings. They are very graceful in the air, twisting and turning as they fly. They eat insects, bathe and drink in flight. All twitter as they fly and many have musical songs. They migrate in flocks for long distances.

The *barn* and *tree swallows* have blue backs and lighter breasts. The *bank* and *rough-winged swallows* have brown backs. In all, tails and wings are darker. The barn swallow

Barn swallows line their nests with feathers

builds its mud nest on a beam under the roof of a barn. The bank swallow digs a nesting hole in the steep bank of a stream or a road. The tree swallow nests in a hole in a tree. Four or five white eggs are laid in the grass and mud nest. The purple MARTIN is the largest of the North American swallows.
                                              E. R. B.

Swallowtail see Butterflies

Swammerdam, Jan (1637-1680) Jan Swammerdam was a Dutch naturalist and biologist (he would now be called a *classical microscopist*) who first described the red blood corpurscles. Of all the microscopists who ever lived, Swammerdam is considered the most accurate and critical. A microscopist is a scientist who studies small plant or animal structures (cells, tissues) under the lens of a microscope.

His first work, *A General History of Insects,* dealt with the various ways insects are transformed and their different modes of development. In fact, almost all his work dealt with minute anatomy in relation to the life history of insects. Swammerdam's *Bible of Nature* is still being used by naturalists, and it contains the finest collection of observations made by means of a microscope ever published.

Born in Amsterdam on February 12, 1637, Swammerdam was the son of a wealthy apothecary and naturalist whose ships sailed to many parts of the world. The natural objects brought back were collected in his father's museum; and young Jan, who helped in the museum, studied interesting animals.

In 1667 he took his medical degree, but neglected his practice for microscopic research. He had been introduced to a microscope as a student and had discovered the red corpuscles of the blood.

While recuperating in the country from malaria, he began to dissect and examine parts of insects under the microscope. He almost blinded himself by working in the bright summer sunlight, but he kept on working. He observed and sketched the intestines of bees, and came to understand the habits of the drones and the queen. He studied the many-faceted eye of the bee, and discovered how the sting worked. His most general work was his study of the process of metamorphosis in insects.

To this day, no one has surpassed Jan Swammerdam in the accuracy and fineness of his work. After his death, his friend Hermann Boerhaave collected his writings and sketches and published them under the title *The Bible of Nature.*   D. H. J.

Courtesy Society For Visual Education, Inc.
Many swamps line the coast of Georgia

Swamp A swamp is an area of low-lying, wet land. Swampland usually has a heavy growth of trees, shrubs, and grasses. The kind of trees, shrubs, and wildlife found in swamps depend on the location of the swamp. The type of soil and amount of drainage also influence the type of growth. Swampy areas are too wet to be used for farming or for grazing animals.

Because swamps and marshes are often found near each other, sometimes these names are used interchangeably. Swamps and marshes are found near seacoasts and along the low shores of ponds, lakes, rivers, and streams. Marshes are different from

Courtesy Society For Visual Education, Inc.
Swamp waters clogged with floating plants

swamps because marshes usually have some shallow water standing on them. Swamps seldom have standing water.

Some swamps have been drained successfully and reclaimed for agricultural purposes. Sometimes an attempt to drain a swamp is a mistake. Some swamps do not have soil that is good enough to make draining worthwhile. The needless draining of swamp areas causes conservation problems. Many wild birds, small animals, reptiles, and insects make their homes or find food in swamps. Some of these wild creatures help to keep down the number of destructive and annoying insects and vermin.   C. L. R.

Swan The swan is a large graceful water bird. Most swans are white. A swan's long neck is curved when it swims and stretched out as it flies. Its plumage is heavy and waterproof. It eats water plants and animals. Swans pair for life. The female nests in a hollow in the ground, using whatever materials are handy and down from her body.

The *whistling swan* is the most common wild swan of the eastern United States. It breeds north of the Arctic Circle and migrates to the southern coast of the United States. The large flocks travel at great heights. As they fly, the swans call in the loud high notes which give them their name. The *trumpeter swan,* once almost extinct, is the heaviest flying bird of North America. The Australian black swan is black with white spots on its wings.   E. R. B.

Swarm see Bee

A white American swan

F. A. Blashfield

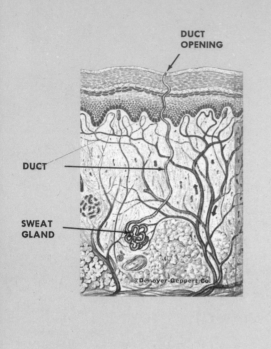

DUCT OPENING

DUCT

SWEAT GLAND

©Denoyer-Geppert Co.

Sweat glands Sweat glands are located under the SKIN of mammals. They are coils of soft, tiny tubes. The tube ends at openings in the skin called *pores*. Sweat glands carry moisture and waste material to the surface of the skin. Sweating, or *perspiring*, helps to keep the body cool.

When moisture evaporates, or goes off into the air, heat is necessary. When the body gets too warm, the amount of warm blood increases in the small capillaries near the surface of the skin. The sweat glands take warm water from the blood and carry it through their tubes or ducts to the pores. When this sweat evaporates, the body is cooler. On humid days, there is much moisture in the air, and the sweat does not evaporate freely. These days are more uncomfortable.

Because sweating takes water from the body, people and animals are thirstier in hot weather, and their bodies need more water. Fevers bring on sweating, too. Physicians often advise feverish patients to drink a lot of water and other fluids.

Sweat glands are most numerous on the palms of the hands and soles of the feet. Furry animals have most of their sweat glands on the pads of their paws.   C. L. K.
SEE ALSO: SKIN MODIFICATIONS

Sweet alyssum see Alyssum

Sweet gum Sweet gum is a tree which grows in southern United States. It produces maple-like leaves, fragrant gum, and valuable hardwood lumber.

Sweet pea Sweet peas are lovely flowers of many colors: blue, lavender, red, orange, white, and pink. They grow on vines. The stem will climb a string attached to a fence.

A sweet pea plant must be grown in the sun in well-drained, well-fertilized soil. The seed of this annual should be sown early in the spring. These fragrant flowers need a cool temperature, for they wither in very hot weather.

The leaf is made up of two narrow leaflets, with climbing tendrils at the end of the leaf stem. The flowers are held erect on strong stems. The blossoms are about an inch long and two inches broad. To keep from injuring the plant, the flowers should be cut after they open and not be plucked. The gray-brown seeds are held in a pod, which is the fruit.   P. G. B.
SEE ALSO: GARDENING, LEGUME

Sweet peas have curled and ruffled petals

Chimney swifts

Sweet potato The sweet potato is a tropical herb grown for its large tuber-like roots. Great amounts of starch and sugar are stored in them. It has been grown as long as corn has.

There are two kinds of sweet potatoes, both in the *morning-glory family*. In one, the root is yellow, dry and mealy. The other is orange, watery and contains more sugar. The first is preferred in the northern states. Sweet potatoes are perennials but are cultivated as annuals. The trailing vines may grow to ten feet long. H. J. C.

Sweet William see Pinks

Sweet potato plant

Sweetbread Sweetbreads are the pancreas (stomach sweetbread) and thymus (neck sweetbread), especially of a calf or lamb, used as food delicacies.

Sweetbriar Sweetbriar or *eglantine,* is a rose with sweet-smelling leaves, pink flowers, and prickly stems. Though of European origin, sweetbriar now grows abundantly in thickets and on roadsides in North America.

Swelling Swelling means an increase in size. Certain solid substances such as gelatin swell in water. Swelling also refers to an enlargement of a part of the body caused by disease or injury. SEE: PATHOLOGY

Swift The swift is a small, grayish-brown bird that flies tirelessly and swiftly. It gives a chattering cry. Swifts are about four to seven inches in length, with wide, curved wings that make them look like a bow and arrow when they fly. They eat flies, mosquitoes and other insects which they catch in flight.

The *chimney swift* is common over eastern North America. Its nest is made of twigs held together and cemented with saliva to the inside of a chimney or old well. Sometimes several birds nest in one chimney. Swifts lay four or five white eggs. The young stay a long time in the nest, sometimes leaving just in time to join the long migratory flight. The *black swift* and *white-throated swift* live along the Pacific Coast. E. R. B.

Swim bladder see Pisces

Swine see Pig

Swiss chard The ancient herb Swiss chard is also called *spinach beet, chard* or *leaf beet.* The leaves or tops of this plant are eaten. They are more highly developed than the roots.

Swiss chard requires a non-acid, rich soil in a cool climate where winters are mild. Seed propagation should be done early in spring. As it grows through the summer, new leaves appear in the center. The outer ones become tough and should be removed. The leaf petioles may grow two feet long and two inches thick.

Swiss chard is rich in vitamins and minerals. A new variety grown has red petioles and gold-green leaves. H. J. C.

Swiss chard, a vegetable

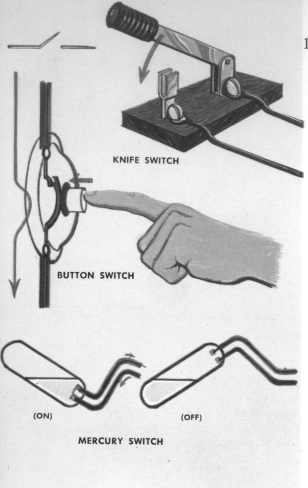

KNIFE SWITCH

BUTTON SWITCH

(ON)   (OFF)

MERCURY SWITCH

Some common types of electric switches

Switches, electric Electric switches are devices for connecting (making) and disconnecting (breaking) electric circuits. Room lights are often controlled by switches on the walls. Lamps have built-in switches. The electric toaster, mixer, stove, iron, and other electrical appliances have switches to turn them on and off.

A simple type of electric switch is the *knife switch*. This switch usually has two knife-like blades. The knife blades have insulated handles. The two blades are connected to two electric wires. The blades fit into metal slots connected to another pair of wires. When the blades are in contact with the slots, the circuit is connected or complete. Electric current then flows through the wires. The knife switch is often used as the main switch at the point where current enters a house or factory.

The *snap* or *toggle* switch is used in electrical appliances and on the walls to control

lights. The current flows from one contact to the other. When the button or lever connected to the switch is pushed one way, the contacts join, allowing the current to flow. When the button or lever is pushed the other way, the current is cut off.

The door bell has a simple type of *push button switch*. When the button is pressed, a strip of brass is pushed down onto a contact point. Thus the circuit is complete.

Mercury switches are being employed more extensively as silent wall switches to control lights. A small amount of mercury is contained in a capsule. When the capsule is tipped, the mercury rolls to one end of the capsule where the two wires are located. There the current flows through the mercury and completes the circuit. When the switch is turned to "off," the mercury moves to the other end of the capsule and breaks the circuit.   P. F. D.

SEE ALSO: ELECTRICITY

Swordfish The swordfish is a long, sleek, fast-swimming fish. Its "sword," actually its upper jaw, is long and pointed, making up one-third of the fish's total length. Sometimes it is called *broadbill* because its sword is flattened, unlike the rounded bill of the MARLIN or sailfish.

The swordfish has no teeth. Its strong sword slashes back and forth through a school of smaller fish, as mackerel or herring, until it kills enough for its meal.

Swordfish travel in pairs through tropical and temperate seas. They are prized as gamefish by sportsmen and harpooned by commercial fishermen for their flavorful meat. Good-sized swordfish are about 400 to 500 pounds. When injured, they become vicious.

Swordfish eggs look like small floating balls. Young swordfish have teeth and scales which they lose as they mature.   C. L. K.

Swordfish, caught for sport or food

Leaves and fruit balls of the sycamore tree

Sycamore (SICK-uh-mohr) One of the easiest ways to identify the sycamore, or *plane tree,* is by the way its inner, smooth, white bark is spotted with patches of older, brown bark. The sycamore grows to be very tall, sometimes over 100 feet. They grow especially well along the banks of rivers.

The broad leaves of the sycamore have from three to five points which are shallower than those of a maple leaf. The underside of the leaf is fuzzy. When the leaf falls, the stem has a hollow space where it fits over the smooth winter bud.

The seed-bearing balls of flowers mature into fruit balls of tightly packed seeds. They dangle on short stems on the bare tree all winter. In spring, the balls break apart into fluff that carries the seeds.

The hard wood of the sycamore makes good butchers' blocks. C. L. K.

Symbiosis see Balance of Nature

Symbol, chemical There are 103 chemical elements known to man. Each element has its own symbol to simplify writing about it. Jakob Berzelius, a Swedish chemist, was the first to use symbols, in the early 1800's.

The simplest method for selecting symbols was to use the first letter of the name of the element, as in the case of hydrogen (H) and oxygen (O). As new elements were discovered, it became necessary to use symbols with more than one letter for elements beginning with the same letter.

Another source of symbols for the elements has been the first letter or two of their Latin names. Among these elements are: sodium (Na), from *natrium;* iron (Fe), from *ferrum;* lead (Pb), from *plumbum.*

In a chemical formula, the symbol of an element represents one atom of that element. When the presence of more than one atom is to be shown, a small number indicating the number of atoms is placed to the right of the symbol. M. S.

SEE ALSO: CHEMISTRY, ELEMENTS, FORMULA, MENDELEEV'S PERIODIC TABLE

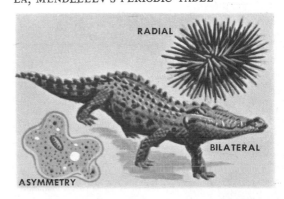

Symmetry, radial and bilateral, and asymmetry

Symmetry (SIMM-uh-tree) Symmetry is the arrangement of the parts of a living organism, either regularly around a central axis (*radial* symmetry); or placed so that right and left body halves are mirror images (*bilateral* symmetry).

SEE: ANIMALS, CLASSIFICATION OF

Sympathetic see Nervous system

Sympton A sympton is a sign indicating the presence of a DISEASE or disorder. PAIN may be a symptom. A change in the appearance or size of an organ may also be a symptom.

SEE: PATHOLOGY

Synapse see Nerve cell

Syndrome (SINN-drohm) A syndrome is a whole set of symptoms and physical signs which occur together and are characteristic of a particular disease. The syndrome, however, does not necessarily describe the disease. Many syndromes help the physician greatly in making correct diagnoses.

Synthesis Synthesis is the combination of parts into a whole. In CHEMISTRY synthesis means the formation of compounds from elements (hydrogen and oxygen make water) or groups of elements (water and quicklime make slaked lime).

Synthetic fabrics Synthetic fabrics are made from fibers which have been created chemically by man. Although they look like natural fibers, many synthetic fibers are stronger, more elastic, and often less expensive to produce. They resist rotting and heat. Synthetic fabrics can be woven to look like cotton, silk, wool, linen, or even fur. Many of these fabrics dry quickly and are easy to care for.

Rayon, acetate, and Arnel, popular clothing and household fabrics, are made from wood cellulose and bits of cotton thread. Spun glass, known for its resistance to fire, acid, rot and heat, is made from sand, limestone and soda. NYLON, used for clothing, tires, carpets, brushes, upholstery, and many other items, is a strong elastic fiber made chiefly from coal, air and water. Natural gas, oil, corn cobs, bran, oats, and rice have also been used in making nylon. Orlon, ACRILAN, and dynel are made from coal, air, water, and limestone. Dacron is made from petroleum and brine; Vinyon is made from soft coal and brine.   D. J. A.
SEE ALSO: COAL TAR

Syphilis Syphilis is a very contagious disease produced by the microorganism spirochetes (Treponema pallida). Infection occurs through contact.

Blossom and fruit of mock orange, a syringa

Syringa (suh-RING-guh) The genus Syringa includes the lilacs, but the common name syringa is widely used for the shrubs often called mock orange. Mock oranges are deciduous—they shed their leaves. They are easily raised and are often used as hedges and screens. They bloom in the late spring and the gracefully curving branches are covered with fragrant white blossoms. The shrub grows to be four to twelve feet tall.

Mock oranges can be planted in the spring or fall. They are raised from seed, layering, or cuttings. They will grow in almost any well-drained soil. Mock oranges like sunshine but will grow in shade better than most flowering shrubs.   M. R. L.
SEE ALSO: CAPSULE, LILAC

System see Anatomy, Physiology

Systole see Heart

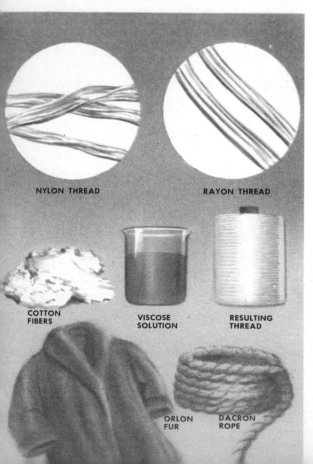

NYLON THREAD

RAYON THREAD

COTTON FIBERS

VISCOSE SOLUTION

RESULTING THREAD

ORLON FUR

DACRON ROPE

First the tadpole's hind legs develop and emerge. The front legs are seen through its skin

Tachometer A tachometer counts the number of revolutions of machinery shafts, usually in a minute. Boat and auto engines, etc., may have gauges which read in RPM.

Tadpole The tadpole is a stage in the development of frogs, salamanders, and toads. A tadpole is a gill breather like the fish. It has a tail which enables it to swim about through the water in which it lives. Sometimes the tadpole is called a "polliwog."

Some animals assume several completely different forms in their development. The tadpole represents a larval stage in the metamorphosis of a FROG. The tadpole develops from the egg looking somewhat like a small fish. After breaking free from the egg membrane, it lives for some days on yolk, and then begins to feed on algae and other small plants. During this early larval stage, it breathes by external gills which are long and branching. Later these gills disappear and internal gills are formed. Water passes from the mouth, over the gill slits, and out of a *spiracle,* or opening, on the tadpole's left side.

At first legs are not present; but later, hind legs appear, and then forelegs. The tail gradually becomes smaller, and the gills are absorbed, as lungs are formed. D. J. I.
SEE ALSO: LARVA, METAMORPHOSIS, SALAMANDER, TOAD

Close-up of a tadpole

Chicago Natural History Museum

Talc The mineral talc is a MAGNESIUM silicate. It is very soft and has a lustrous, waxlike, pearly finish. In color it is white to gray or green. When rolled between the fingers, it feels greasy. Most tailors' chalk is composed of talc.

Tallow Tallow is a mixture of hard fats. It is extracted from the natural fat of sheep and cattle by melting the animal fat in water and skimming the tallow off the surface. It is used in margarine, soap, and candles.
SEE: FAT

Tamarack (TAMM-uh-rack) Tamarack is a tree of the PINE group. Tamaracks are sometimes called American larches or hackmatacks. These trees are valuable for their timber.

Tamarack trees grow about sixty-five feet tall. They have the shape of a long, narrow cone. The leaves are about an inch long and are slender and blunt. They drop these needle-like leaves in the fall. They are usually found in acid soil. M. R. L.

Tamarau see Water buffalo

Tamarack tree

Scarlet tanagers have large yellow bills

Tanager The tanager is a beautifully colored American bird. It is six or seven inches long and stocky. It feeds on insects found on leaves or in flight. Its call is a hoarse, buzzy warble. Most tanagers build shallow nests of twigs and weeds near the ends of branches. The eggs are blue, green or purple with brownish markings at one end.

The *scarlet tanager* lives in woody eastern and central United States. The male has black wings and tail; the rest of the bird is a bright orange-red. The female is a drab greenish-yellow.

The *western tanager* is yellow except for a red head and black wings and tail. The *summer tanager* of the Southeast is all red. All male tanagers molt their red plumage and become yellowish in the fall.   E. R. B.

Tangerine see Citrus fruit

Tannin (TANN-inn) Tannins, or tannic acids as they are sometimes called, are substances obtained from a number of plants, such as the oak and sumac. They are used in the manufacture of leather, dyes, and ink. Tannins are soluble in water, and have a taste like lemon juice or other acid material.

SEE: ECONOMIC BOTANY, LEATHER

Tanning see Leather

Tantalum (TANN-tuh-luhm) Tantalum is the 73rd element. It is usually found in ores in combination with niobium. This metal can be made in almost pure form. It is gray in color. Although it is very hard, it can be drawn into fine wires and shaped into many forms.

Tantalum is very resistant to chemical attack, and will react only with the very corrosive hydrofluoric acid and with solid alkalies. Tantalum is used in surgery to cover skull defects, since it is the only metal known on which flesh will adhere and grow.

Tantalum (symbol Ta) has atomic weight 180.948 (180.95, O = 16). It forms compounds of chlorides and fluorides.   M. S.

SEE ALSO: ATOM, ELEMENTS

Tapeworm Tapeworms are long, ribbon-like *parasites*. This means that they live in the bodies of other animals. They take food and shelter from their host. In return, they offer only illness.

Most tapeworms live in the bodies of *vertebrates* (animals with backbones). All adult tapeworms live in the intestines of their hosts. Since food is easy to find there, tapeworms have neither mouths nor digestive systems. Tapeworms belong to the *flatworm* group.

The life cycle of the tapeworm is complicated. In order to develop from an egg to an embryo and finally to an adult, the tapeworm must find two different hosts. Since it is not able, at any stage of its development, to move independently from place to place, it must rely upon unsanitary conditions in order to transfer eggs from one host to another.

The *beef tapeworm* displays a typical life cycle. The eggs which fall on the grass are

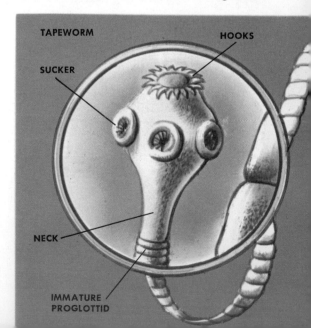

TAPEWORM

HOOKS

SUCKER

NECK

IMMATURE PROGLOTTID

Buchsbaum

eaten by the cow. In the intestine of the cow, the eggshell is digested off and the embryo is released. After boring its way through the intestinal wall, the embryo enters the bloodstream and is carried to a muscle where it remains. It develops into a sac, or *bladder*, containing a head. When man, the second host, eats uncooked beef containing the bladder, the embryo head attaches itself to the intestinal walls and develops into an adult. The mature tapeworm produces eggs that are eliminated from the intestine with the feces or waste materials.

A tapeworm is often described as made up of sacks of reproductive organs. Since the transfer of eggs from one host to the next is so chancy, the major activity of the tapeworm is that of producing eggs. As many as 1000 a day may be produced by one adult.

The tapeworm is made up of individual sections called *proglottids*. These are joined together behind a head or *scolex*. Since new sections are budded off behind the head, the most mature sections are at the end of the body. Within each proglottid, a complete set of male and female organs develops. After the eggs are fertilized, the sex organs degenerate, the eggs mature, and the "ripe" sections detach from the worm and pass out with the feces.

Like most parasites, the tapeworm adapts itself to a parasitic way of life by losing or changing many of its structures. The digestive system disappears and the muscular and nervous systems are reduced. The outer covering of cells secretes a thick, protective cuticle.

E. P. L.

SEE ALSO: PARASITE, PLATYHELMINTHES

Tapir (TA-purr) The tapir is a shy, hoofed mammal that lives in the thick forests of Malaya and South America. It feeds at night on fruit and leaves. Since the tapir likes to roll in mud and bathe in rivers, it lives near water.

The almost hairless and tailless tapir is about the size of a large pig. In body and head shape, it resembles the pig. Instead of a snout, it has a short trunk. Except for the Malayan tapir, which has a white back, the adult tapir is black-brown in color. The young of all species have light spots and stripes similar to those of the wild pig.

The tapir is a hoofed mammal called an *ungulate*. The four toes on each front foot and

Buchsbaum

The stripes and spots of the young tapir fade as it grows. Adults are a solid brown-black color

the three toes on each back foot are enclosed in individual hoofs. Since the third toe is the largest, the tapir is known as an *odd-toed ungulate* or *perissodactyl*, along with the horse and rhinoceros.

Tapirs are often called *living fossils*. Fossil tapirs, which date back 70 million years, were similar to living tapirs. These animals have shown fewer evolutionary changes than have other hoofed mammals, as the horse. E. P. L.

Taproot see Root

Tar Tar is a brownish-black, sticky substance obtained by DISTILLATION of organic materials such as wood, waste fats, petroleum, coal and peat. Tars have wide uses, such as for road surfacing, paints and other wood preservatives, and for sealing roofs.

Distilled coal and PETROLEUM give tars having an alkaline reaction, but wood tars are slightly acid.

A variety of substances made from tars include dyes, perfumes, drugs, insecticides, explosives, moth balls, a germicide (pyridine), carbolic acid, an artificial sweetener, pitch, film and photographic chemicals, and some plastics. D. C. H.

SEE ALSO: COAL TAR

Tarantula see Arachnida, Spiders

Tarnish see Rusting

Taro tuber and "elephant's ear" leaves

Taro (TAH-roh) Taro is a tropical food plant. It is a favorite starchy food in many oriental countries and in Polynesia, in the Hawaiian Islands and other Pacific islands. It is cultivated in the southern United States for its edible starchy tubers. The *elephant's ear* is a well-known species of taro found in many American gardens. This ornamental plant grows enormous leaves in just a few weeks. The leaves of the elephant's ear are shield or heart-shaped, and may be three feet long. They have attractive purple margins and veins.

Taro is a large, potato-like tuber. It contains an easily digested starch, and can be boiled or baked in a way that will eliminate the bitter flavor of its juice. Taro sprouts are gathered outdoors in the spring and are known as *dasheen*. They are prepared like asparagus. In the winter they may be forced and served in the same way. *Poi* is a traditional and world-famous Hawaiian dish made from taro that has been ground to a paste and then fermented. The large leaves of taro are also cooked and eaten. M. R. L.

Tarpon The tarpon is a large, silvery game fish that belongs to the HERRING order. It may weigh as much as 300 pounds, and is found in the warmer waters of the Atlantic.

Tarpon is a game fish

Tarragon Tarragon perennial European herb is related to *sagebrush*. Its sweet-smelling leaves are used for seasoning vinegar, sauces, salads, and soups.
SEE: SPICE

Tarsier see Primates

Taste Taste is one of the six senses. The areas for tasting are usually found around the mouth and nose. Most mammals have four kinds of taste sensations—*bitter, sweet, sour* or *acid,* and *salty*. Cells, mainly on the tongue, pick up the stimulus when food is dissolved. A dry object on a dry tongue has no taste.

Taste cells are found in other places in the mouth as on the soft and hard palates, epiglottis, tonsils and walls of the throat. These places, however, have very few in relation to the number on the tongue, which probably has up to 10,000 taste buds. The related areas of taste are more evident in youngsters, so that as one ages one declines in the ability to taste.

The tongue has minute projections on it called *papillae*. Embedded in the mucous membrane between these little mounds are bundles of cells which form a *taste bud*. The particular cells are long and narrow. The ends of the cells at the surface of the tongue have tiny hairs or *cilia*. They are exposed to the outside by a small opening called the *taste pore*. The other end of these elongated cells are in contact with the dendrites of neurons. The sensation is passed from the cilia through the cells to a cranial nerve which carries a stimulus to the taste center in the cerebrum. Here one interprets it as salty, sweet, bitter or sour.

The sense of taste is very closely associated with the sense of smell. That is why a person with a bad cold, whose nasal passages are blocked, cannot taste his food well.

Most vertebrates have taste areas in the mouth but some invertebrates can pick up taste stimuli over various parts of their bodies. Certain insects, for example, have front legs more useful to detecting taste than any part of the mouth. H. J. C.
SEE ALSO: SENSE ORGANS

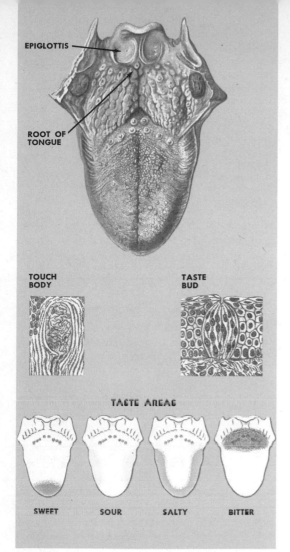

TASTE AREAS

SWEET   SOUR   SALTY   BITTER

©Denoyer-Geppert Co.

Taurus, the Bull

Taurus (TAWR-uhs) Taurus, the bull, is the second sign of the ZODIAC. It is one of the most distinctly marked of the constellations, and is readily observed in the winter months. It rises in the eastern sky, to the north of ORION and contains 145 stars. Easily recognized parts are the *Pleiades* and the *Hyades*.

The Pleiades, or Seven Sisters, form a tiny dipper-shape, so small that it is blacked out by the tip of a finger held at arm's length. Nonetheless, six of the stars can be seen with the naked eye. The Hyades lie near in the shape of an isosceles triangle, which is open at the end. It is bright and very regular in shape. Associated with it is *Aldebaran,* a reddish-colored, first magnitude star, considered the bull's eye.

In mythology, the Pleiades were the seven daughters of Atlas who were transformed into a group of stars—the seventh, or invisible one (to the naked eye), is the "lost" star hiding in shame because she loved a mortal. The Hyades were half-sisters of the Pleiades. They wept because of their brother Hyas' death, a myth which probably developed because in parts of Europe their advent, or appearance, marks the beginning of a rainy season.   D. J. A.

SEE ALSO: CONSTELLATION

Taxidermy (TAX-sih-der-mee) Taxidermy is the process or science by which animals are preserved and prepared for display or study. The methods vary for different kinds of animals. Great skill is needed, as well as knowledge of the *anatomy* or structure of the animals being prepared.

The word taxidermy means "sorting skins"; but it includes much more than sorting, arranging, and preparing the animals. It involves the setting up of natural-appearing habitats and display arrangements so that the animals appear to be in the proper surroundings. This is most important to the "real as life" look of the animal groups seen in museums today.

Taxidermy once meant stuffing dead animals. Although some of this was done to preserve trophies of the hunt, the art of taxidermy was furthered most by those interested in developing collections for commercial or educational purposes. Work in this field was done in the 19th century in France. Later, in America, advancement was made in taxidermy procedures. Professor Henry Ward set up an establishment in Rochester, New York, to supply specimens to institutions throughout the country. Today, taxidermy work is largely an activity

HOW TO STUFF AN ANIMAL

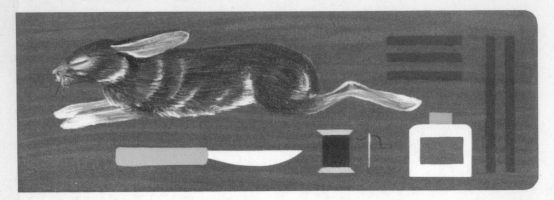

This experience is for young students of science interested in contributing to a collection for a school museum. Many vertebrates may be stuffed for a comparative study.

1   Begin with a freshly killed animal. An adult should supervise the use of chloroform.

2   Separate the fur, feathers, or other covering when cutting through the skin. When the animal is sewn back up the coat will cover the incision.

3   Skin the animal as carefully as possi-ble. Rub borax powder into the hide on both sides and permit it to stand for several hours before removing.

4   It will be necessary to cut off the appendages and skull. Soak these in borax solution overnight.

5   Stuff the trunk with cotton. Fasten dowel rods to the appendages and insert them into the original openings. Sew up the incision in the pelt.

6   Small buttons can be painted to mimic eyes. Glue them into the sockets.

carried on by museums, universities, and the present Ward establishment.

Techniques for preparing different kinds of animals vary. *Mammals* and *birds* are generally skinned, and the skins stretched and sewn onto models. In the case of *fish* and *reptiles,* because of the changeability and tendency of the skins to crack, artificial reproductions made from the original animals are frequently developed. These are usually more lifelike and always more durable than the real skins would be.

A general procedure in all taxidermy is to take accurate measurements of all parts of the body, and detailed notes on the colors of parts, eyes, and so on. Later these are needed for adding the final realistic touches.

Small mammals and birds are similarly treated. They are cleaned of debris. The skin is carefully separated from the body, usually by being cut from the ventral side. The bones are fleshed and cleaned for display or other use. Chemicals, such as powdered borax, are rubbed on bird skins as they are stripped, in order to preserve them. The skin is later water-washed and treated for preservation. In the same way, small mammal skins are cleaned and tanned. This permits them to endure indefinitely.

Balsa models are prepared from dimensions of the original animal. Padding of various materials is used where necessary. The skin is stretched over the form. Wire is used to support birds' wings and other parts. Glass eyes are used in place of natural ones. Final fluffing of feathers or fur and touching up with colors and it is ready for display.

In the preparation of larger mammals, a different procedure is necessary. Molds of plaster of Paris are often made directly, in addition to the taking of measurements from the freshly killed animal. These aid later in giving the specimen a natural appearance. The skin is carefully removed. The skin is salted to preserve it, and left a few days before it is tanned. The bones are stripped of muscles and cleaned to be used in displays or for other purposes. When ready, the bones are assembled as they were in the living animal. A clay model which duplicates the original animal body is made around the skeleton. This leaves a good but clumsy, heavy specimen. Around this is made a plaster mold. When dry, sections of it are separated. Layers of burlap are glued in, and iron rods are anchored within to provide later support. This forms what is called the *mannikin*. It is well made since it will be the specimen's final body. The molds are wired together and the mannikin within is allowed to dry for a few days. When it is ready, the mold is cut and broken away. The mannikin is then sewn together and finished. The skin is stretched and sewn over it, and final arranging and positioning are done.

In the case of fish, several procedures are used. The earlier one involved skinning of the fish and building a model of the body. An alternative was to use a mold of the original fish (by making a plaster cast), over which was stretched the skin. This gives a good specimen except that in passing years the skin may crack. A preferable method is to make casts in plaster from molds taken of the original fish. These, when painted realistically, are a durable and accurate, if artificial, representation of the original.

Reptiles are sometimes prepared as fish are. There is a better method which is used for many of them, as well as for other kinds of animals. It is especially effective where color has to show through *translucently* from within. Many animals with bare skin like snakes, turkey heads, or *hippopotami*, have in real life a color quality which disappears in skin preparation. A plastic model is made of them. First, a plaster cast is made of parts or of the whole dead animal. It is done with extreme care, with the animal's position as it is desired for final display. The sections are then separated. With infinite care, liquid plastic is applied to the inside of the mold. (Imagine painting a water glass from within.) Appropriate colors are added to the plastic and painted on. This is a painstaking task since the building up of color layers takes place gradually. Because the color layers are applied from the model's inside, each layer will show through as the final coloration of the animal.

When all colored plastic is layered in, a center filler is put in for strength. After drying, the outside plaster mold is wet and broken away. This method gives the most realistic results for reptiles.   D. J. I.

Taxonomy see Anatomy; Animals, classification of; Evolution; Plants, classification of

REINFORCING RODS AND BOARDS FORM THE PRIMARY SKELETON OR FOUNDATION TO SIMULATE THE GORILLA

THE BODY IS THEN BUILT UP AND FASHIONED WITH CLAY. WHEN WELL-ROUNDED AND LIFE-LIKE IN SIZE, THE SKIN IS FITTED FOR SIZE AND REMOVED

NEXT A COAT OF CLAY IS PLACED OVER THE MOLD, ALLOWED TO DRY AND THEN CUT OFF IN SECTIONS AND REINFORCED AND BRACED

WHEN THE REINFORCED PLASTER LIKENESS IS ASSEMBLED, THE SKIN IS GLUED IN PLACE

Tea Tea is an evergreen shrub or tree grown for its leaves. When they are dried and put into hot water, they make a beverage. Tea is native to the Orient and was first used as medicine. It is now grown in some of the southern states. The tea family includes the flowering CAMELLIA. The scientific name of the family is *Theaceae*.

The tea plant grows from five to 30 feet depending on the degree of pruning. The leaves are two to five inches long, serrated, leathery and possessing oil glands. The flower is white to pink and develops into a capsule fruit.

The kind and quality of tea depends on several factors. The new young leaves make the best drink, called *golden tips* and *orange pekoe*. The larger leaves produce a poorer grade. The older the plant, the more bitter the leaves become. Green tea is made from dried,

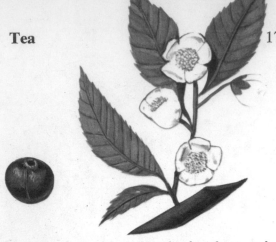

Tea leaves are picked, then dried or fermented

rolled green leaves. If these same leaves were permitted to ferment, black tea would be produced.

Tea contains three useful chemicals—*essential oil, tannin* and *theine.* The last one is a stimulant. When tea is brewed too long, the tannin dissolves and is freed, making the tea bitter. H. J. C.

SEE ALSO: ECONOMIC BOTANY

Teak (TEEK) The teak is a tall, large, tropical tree well-known for its strong wood. The teak wood contains a fragrant oil that preserves wood and metals from rust and decay. Teakwood is used in shipbuilding, furniture, and in making chests and beautifully carved ornaments.

Teak grows in Thailand, India, and Burma, and neighboring areas. The trees may grow 200 feet tall, with oval leaves over one foot long. A red or purple dye is sometimes made from the leaves. The wood is rare and highly prized. M. R. L.

Teal see Duck

Wood of the teak tree has an attractive grain

Tears Tears are a watery liquid bathing the eyeball. They keep the surface of the eyeball moist and clean. Tears are always being produced and drained away. They drain through the nose (*nasolacrimal canal*) from ducts (*lacrimal*) at the corner of the eye nearest the nose. In weeping so many tears are produced at one time that they do not drain away fast enough and spill out of the eye.

SEE: EYE

Technetium (teck-NEE-shum) Technetium is a chemical element. It is not radioactively stable, that is, it does not have a stable ISOTOPE, and so is not found in nature. Technetium was formerly called *masurium.*

Technetium is related to MANGANESE and RHENIUM, and is in the same group in the periodic table. Thus chemically, it behaves like these elements. It has metallic properties. Technetium is produced by nuclear bombardment of MOLYBDENUM atoms or as a *fission* product of uranium-235.

Technetium (symbol Tc) has atomic number 43. Its most stable isotope has mass number 99. It forms compounds with oxygen and most of its radioactive isotopes have very short half-lives. D. J. I.

SEE ALSO: ATOM, ELEMENTS

Technicolor see Motion pictures

Technology Technology is applied science and industrial art. It takes the discoveries and inventions of scientists and makes them available in practical form for man. It supplies the needs of mankind with tools and machines.

Through mass production, machines produce goods faster and cheaper and, in many instances, better than can be made by hand. A machine, driven by steam, electric, or atomic energy can make products which cannot be produced by hand. Synthetic dyes, drugs, foods, clothes, fuels, cars, airplanes, and ships are only a very few products made possible by technology. D. A. B.

SEE ALSO: SCIENCE

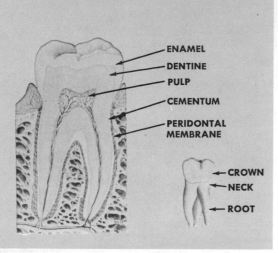

ENAMEL
DENTINE
PULP
CEMENTUM
PERIDONTAL MEMBRANE

← CROWN
← NECK
← ROOT

UPPER

PERMANENT TEETH

1—CENTRAL INCISORS
2—LATERAL INCISORS
3—CANINES
4—FIRST BICUSPIDS
5—SECOND BICUSPIDS
6—FIRST MOLARS
7—SECOND MOLARS
8—THIRD MOLARS

LOWER

TODAY'S HEALTH, published by AMERICAN MEDICAL ASSOCIATION

Teeth All mammals use their teeth to chew food. Many other animals also have these bony organs in their mouth. Teeth may be used to grab, hold and tear food. They may serve for protection, such as the poison fangs of a rattlesnake. The walrus uses its tusks to drag its body along rocky shores. Beavers use their sharp teeth to cut down trees to build homes. Some animals are toothless. Birds, toads, turtles, some fish and a small community of men in India do not have a tooth in their heads.

Humans have two sets of teeth. *Baby,* or *temporary,* teeth begin to appear in about the sixth month. By the time a child is two years old, he usually has all twenty. The second set, or *permanent teeth,* are buried in the gums beneath the temporary ones. At this stage they are much smaller than they will be eventually. When the child is about six years old, the permanent teeth begin to push the baby teeth out. This process will continue for six years (twenty years for wisdom teeth) until an adult has 32 permanent teeth. The *dental formula* (2-1-2-3) refers to the number of kind of teeth in each one half of each jaw. Man has two *incisors,* one *canine,* two *bicuspids,* and three *molars.*

Though teeth vary in size and shape, their internal structure is similar. The *crown* is that portion extending out from the gums. It is composed of *dentine,* a dense bony material, which is covered by hard *enamel.* The crown tapers to the *neck* and finally into one or more hollow roots. The opening at the base of the root permits blood vessels and nerves to enter the pulp cavity.

The proper development of teeth depends upon numerous factors. Since the composition of teeth is high in calcium, phosphorus and other minerals, the diet of an animal is very important. Vitamins A, B, D are essential. FLUORINE is helpful in maintaining clean and healthy teeth. An insufficient supply of hormones from some endocrine glands, THYROID and PARATHYROID, will affect the normal growth of strong teeth. Certain chemicals will cause the calcium salts in enamel to become soluble and start decay. One such action will occur when bacteria digest carbohydrates and give off acids.

Teeth aid the whole process of digestion in a number of ways. Chewing food makes it easier to swallow and adds moisture to dry foods. It permits the saliva carrying the enzyme *ptyalin* to become thoroughly mixed with all parts of the food.

Teeth have been part of the animal body almost from the beginning of animal life. Among the invertebrates, the HOOKWORM has platelike teeth to help suck blood. The teeth of CHITON in leeches help obtain food from their hosts. Snails have a radula of teeth to scrape plants. Crayfish have teeth in their stomachs that are used for grinding. Mammals have two sets and a definite number of teeth. Rodents' teeth are open at the base of the root to allow for continued growth. They keep wearing them down from constant gnawing. Most of the teeth of pigs are present at birth. The largest tooth in history was in an extinct mammoth. It measured 16 feet long and weighed over 250 pounds.   H. J. C.

SEE ALSO: TOOTH DECAY

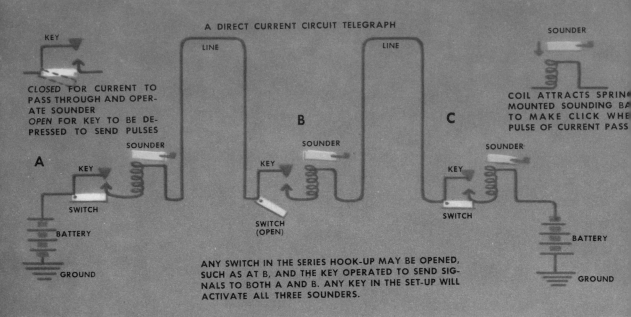

A DIRECT CURRENT CIRCUIT TELEGRAPH

KEY

CLOSED FOR CURRENT TO PASS THROUGH AND OPERATE SOUNDER
OPEN FOR KEY TO BE DEPRESSED TO SEND PULSES

A

SWITCH

BATTERY

GROUND

LINE

SOUNDER

KEY

B

SOUNDER

KEY

SWITCH
(OPEN)

LINE

SOUNDER

C

KEY

SWITCH

ANY SWITCH IN THE SERIES HOOK-UP MAY BE OPENED, SUCH AS AT B, AND THE KEY OPERATED TO SEND SIGNALS TO BOTH A AND B. ANY KEY IN THE SET-UP WILL ACTIVATE ALL THREE SOUNDERS.

SOUNDER

COIL ATTRACTS SPRING MOUNTED SOUNDING BAR TO MAKE CLICK WHEN PULSE OF CURRENT PASS

SOUNDER

BATTERY

GROUND

Telegraph Telegraph is an instrument of communication. Messages are sent and received by signals made by connecting and breaking an electric circuit. Before telegraphy, messages could not be sent quickly.

There are basically two kinds of telegraphy—*line* or *wire telegraphy* and *wireless* or *radiotelegraphy*. In wire telegraphy the sending and receiving stations are connected by a direct wire. In radiotelegraphy, the telegraph signals are sent out from a special RADIO transmitter and picked up on a special radio receiver. There is no wire connecting the sending and receiving stations. Wire telegraphy is used by the Western Union system, by railroads, by many large companies which have direct wires between their branch offices, and by the military services. Radiotelegraphy is used for ship-to-shore communication and in many military installations.

The wire telegraph originally consisted of a *sending key,* which opened and closed the circuit, and a *sounder* connected by wires to the key. The voltage was supplied by a battery. When the circuit was closed by the key, an iron bar was attracted in the electromagnet of the sounder. When the circuit was opened, the bar was pulled away by a spring. When the bar hit the electromagnet, it produced a click. These clicks were varied according to the *Morse code.*

Although key circuits are still used in places, most wire lines are *teletypewriter* lines. Both sending and receiving points have a device which resembles a typewriter,

but the keyboard only has capitals and numerals on it. The message is typed on this teletypewriter, which automatically transmits each letter as a series of pulses. A different pulse pattern represents each letter, much as a different combination of dots and dashes represents each letter in code.

The receiving unit converts the electrical pulses back to mechanical energy and the message is automatically typed out.

When the same message must be sent to many receivers, a unit is used which perforates a paper tape. This perforated tape is inserted into a device which converts the perforations into electrical pulses to be sent over wire or fed to a radio transmitter.

In radiotelegraphy, the transmitted wave is modulated (altered) so it can carry a message. Modulation is imposed by opening and closing a circuit, either by a key or with a teletypewriter tape.

The telegraph was not the contribution of one man. One of the contributors was James Maxwell, who, in 1831, studied and clarified the theory of *electromagnetism*. He and a German scientist, Henry Hertz, experimented with electromagnetic waves. An inventor named David Hughes learned to detect electromagnetic waves, using a gap in his spark transmitter. In 1831, MICHAEL FARADAY discovered *electrical inductance*. Later, the Italian electrical engineer MARCONI improved the wireless telegraph so that it would transmit signals for longer distances.

Two Americans, JOSEPH HENRY and Samuel F. Morse, also contributed greatly to the development of the telegraph. E. Y. K.
SEE ALSO: ELECTROMAGNET; INDUCTION; MORSE, SAMUEL

✳ THINGS TO DO

SENDING MESSAGES BY CODE

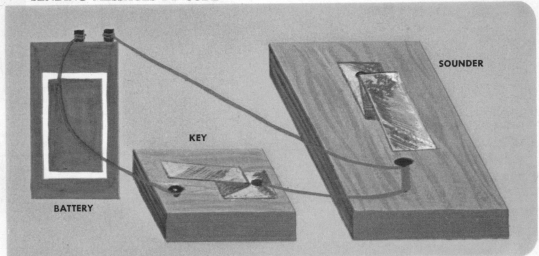

1 Assemble an electromagnet by wrapping bell wire around a screw at least twenty turns. Screw the electromagnet into a small board.

2 Cut a strip of metal from a tin can. Make it one inch wide and two inches longer than the length of the screw. This will serve as the armature when fastened near the electromagnet. Follow the diagram. You have just constructed a telegraph sounder.

3 Assemble a telegraph key or switch with a second small board, screw, and metal strip. Bend the key upwards as shown in the illustration.

4 The two free ends of bell wire leading from the telegraph sounder should be connected to the screw on the switch and to one terminal on the dry cell. A third wire connects the other terminal to the screw holding the key.

5 Learn the Morse code from the table below and with a friend send messages back and forth.

INTERNATIONAL MORSE CODE

A ·—	N —·	1 ·————	6 —····
B —···	O ———	2 ··———	7 ——···
C —·—·	P ·——·	3 ···——	8 ———··
D —··	Q ——·—	4 ····—	9 ————·
E ·	R ·—·	5 ·····	0 —————
F ··—·	S ···		
G ——·	T —		
H ····	U ··—	Period ·—·—·—	
I ··	V ···—	Comma ——··——	
J ·———	W ·——	SOS ···———···	
K —·—	X —··—	Start —·—	
L ·—··	Y —·——	End of message ·—·—·	
M ——	Z ——··	Error ········	

Alexander Graham Bell and his original model of the telephone

Telephone Since Alexander Bell invented the telephone in 1876, it has become the most important means of COMMUNICATION. It can send the sound of a voice to any receiver on the same line, and the line from a telephone can be connected to almost any telephone in the world. RADIO and TELEVISION networks use telephone lines to send their programs between stations. The telephone system uses radio to send calls overseas to any country with a telephone system.

The telephone sends and receives sound on wires, or lines, by changing the sound to electric pulses. The telephone headset has a *receiver* and a *transmitter*. The transmitter that Bell used in his first working telephone was crude. The same method has been refined and is used in modern telephones to change sound vibrations into electric impulses. Bell knew that sound vibrations could produce similar vibrations in any solid object. He experimented with a thin metal reed attached to a simple switch. The switch was connected to a battery and a receiver. He found that this transmitter could not send a human voice, and he looked for another method of controlling the battery current.

He attached a thin metal *diaphragm* to a tiny box filled with carbon granules. The carbon box was connected so that it completed the telephone line circuit back to the battery.

Carbon black, or soot, is a poor conductor used in *resistors;* but it can be finely divided. It will conduct better when it is compressed than when it is loosely packed. In Bell's transmitter, the diaphragm is alternately pushed and pulled by the sound vibrations; and the carbon granules are pushed closer together and farther apart in the same way. The diaphragm simply acts as a sound-sensitive surface, but the carbon box actually changes the battery current into electric pulses that copy the sound impulses. The important difference between the carbon telephone transmitter and the simple switch that Bell discarded is that the switch turns the current completely on or off, while his ingenious carbon box could change the current continuously from zero to maximum. It could send a sound which has several frequencies, such as the complex human voice.

In reproducing a voice, Bell used another principle. He used electromagnets in a receiver to change the electric pulses back into sound. He connected the electromagnet coils to the telephone line, and mounted a diaphragm at one end of the coils so that it could vibrate slightly. When current flowed in the electromagnet, the steel diaphragm pulled toward it, and was released when the current stopped. In this way the diaphragm vibrated to reproduce the sound picked up by the transmitter.

In a system with more than two sets of transmitters and receivers, some switching system must be used to send a call to a selected station. In the modern telephone

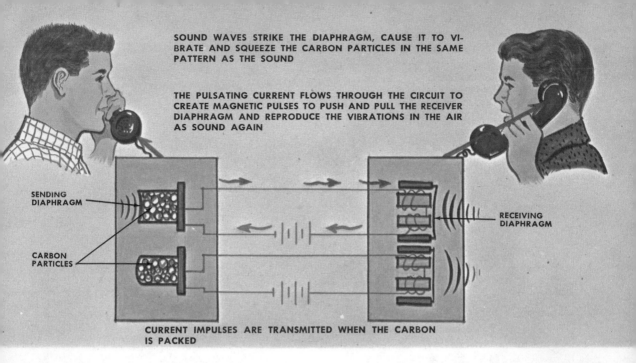

SOUND WAVES STRIKE THE DIAPHRAGM, CAUSE IT TO VIBRATE AND SQUEEZE THE CARBON PARTICLES IN THE SAME PATTERN AS THE SOUND

THE PULSATING CURRENT FLOWS THROUGH THE CIRCUIT TO CREATE MAGNETIC PULSES TO PUSH AND PULL THE RECEIVER DIAPHRAGM AND REPRODUCE THE VIBRATIONS IN THE AIR AS SOUND AGAIN

SENDING DIAPHRAGM

RECEIVING DIAPHRAGM

CARBON PARTICLES

CURRENT IMPULSES ARE TRANSMITTED WHEN THE CARBON IS PACKED

system, switches are the most numerous components. The vast system of lines, relays, crossbar switches, and computers took more than 50 years to develop. All calls are switched through two types of offices—the local, or exchange, office; and the regional office, which handles the interexchange and long distance calls. Most exchange offices now use an automatic dialing system instead of an operator, but a few rural areas still use manual switching.

Before 1913, the first dialing systems were used by small independent companies. By 1930, the Bell telephone dialing system automatically connected phones within the exchange areas. The long distance calls were relayed from exchange to exchange by operators using trunk lines. Now, any number in the United States can be directly dialed if his exchange has been connected into the direct dialing trunks.   D. A. B.

SEE ALSO: BELL, ALEXANDER GRAHAM; ELECTROMAGNET; SOUND; VOICE

Telephotography In telephotography, photographs are "sensed" by a system of photoelectric cells as a light beam is scanned across them. Depending upon the brightness of the reflected light, a current can be amplified and sent over wire circuits or radio. Long range lenses, *telescopes,* enable photographs to be made on film.

SEE: PHOTOELECTRICITY, PHOTOGRAPHY

Principle of telephotography

FACSIMILE

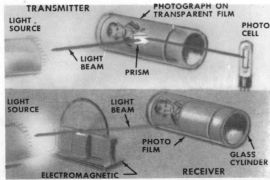

TRANSMITTER

LIGHT SOURCE

PHOTOGRAPH ON TRANSPARENT FILM

PHOTO CELL

LIGHT BEAM

PRISM

LIGHT SOURCE

LIGHT BEAM

PHOTO FILM

GLASS CYLINDER

ELECTROMAGNETIC

RECEIVER

✳ **THINGS TO DO**

MAKING A REFRACTING TELESCOPE

1 Locate two long cardboard tubes, one slightly smaller in circumference.
2 Two lens (one of long focal length and one of short) are needed which match the diameter of the tubes. Fasten one in the opposite end of each tube.

3 When the smaller tube is placed into the larger tube you are ready to observe. Move the smaller tube in and out until the object is clear.
4 Is the picture upside down? Use your telescope at night. Can you see stars better than with the naked eye?

Telescope A telescope is an instrument that is used to observe and study distant objects. It is one of the most important tools of the astronomer.

The main function of a telescope is to bring into view objects that are so faint they cannot be seen with the naked eye. Telescopes also magnify distant objects. They can separate objects, such as double stars, that are so close together that they appear as one to the naked eye, and more detail can be seen on distant objects.

The telescope consists of a long tube holding lenses, or mirrors and lenses, the proper distances apart to collect light waves from a distant object and form a visible image of it.

There are two main types of telescopes: *refracting* telescopes and *reflecting* telescopes. In a refracting telescope, a large *convex* lens is situated at the top of a long tube. This "object glass" collects the nearly parallel light waves from a distant object and bends, or refracts, the waves to form an image farther down inside the tube. A simple experiment with a magnifying glass shows how this principle of refraction works. If a magnifying glass (a lens) is held a few inches away from a piece of paper so that the sun shines directly on the lens, an image of the sun will be formed on the paper. In a telescope this image is not focused on a screen for viewing by the eye. Instead, another lens, the *eyepiece,* is situated at the bottom of the tube. The eyepiece magnifies the image formed within the tube by the object glass and focuses the light waves into the image that the observer sees.

Reflecting telescopes use *mirrors* to *reflect* light instead of lenses that refract it. A re-

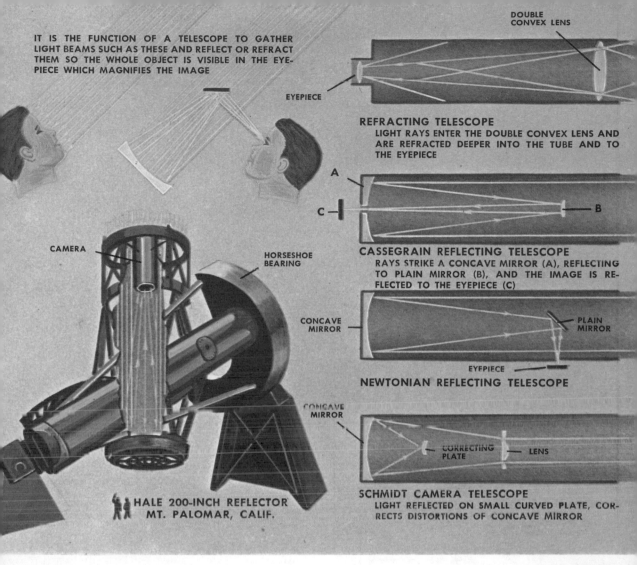

IT IS THE FUNCTION OF A TELESCOPE TO GATHER LIGHT BEAMS SUCH AS THESE AND REFLECT OR REFRACT THEM SO THE WHOLE OBJECT IS VISIBLE IN THE EYEPIECE WHICH MAGNIFIES THE IMAGE

EYEPIECE

DOUBLE CONVEX LENS

REFRACTING TELESCOPE
LIGHT RAYS ENTER THE DOUBLE CONVEX LENS AND ARE REFRACTED DEEPER INTO THE TUBE AND TO THE EYEPIECE

A
C
B

CASSEGRAIN REFLECTING TELESCOPE
RAYS STRIKE A CONCAVE MIRROR (A), REFLECTING TO PLAIN MIRROR (B), AND THE IMAGE IS REFLECTED TO THE EYEPIECE (C)

CAMERA
HORSESHOE BEARING
CONCAVE MIRROR
PLAIN MIRROR
EYEPIECE

NEWTONIAN REFLECTING TELESCOPE

CONCAVE MIRROR
CORRECTING PLATE
LENS

HALE 200-INCH REFLECTOR MT. PALOMAR, CALIF.

SCHMIDT CAMERA TELESCOPE
LIGHT REFLECTED ON SMALL CURVED PLATE, CORRECTS DISTORTIONS OF CONCAVE MIRROR

flecting telescope consists of a large hollow tube at the bottom of which is a *concave* mirror. The mirror reflects the light waves and focuses them in an image near the top of the tube. A second, plain mirror reflects this image so that it can be seen with the eyepiece near the top of the telescope.

The degree of magnification of a telescope is determined by the *focal length* of the eyepiece and by the focal length of the objective lens. There is a practical limit to the degree of magnification of any telescope. The larger the objective lens, the greater the magnification that can be achieved without fuzziness.

The largest reflecting telescope is the 200-inch Hale reflector on Mount Palomar in California. The largest refractor is at Yerkes Observatory in Wisconsin. The object glass of the Yerkes refractor is 40 inches across. This is about as big as a refracting telescope can be because the lens of a refractor can only be supported around it edges. A larger lens would sag and lose its shape.

The refracting telescope was invented around 1600 by Hans Lippershey, an eyeglass maker from Holland. GALILEO was the first person to use the refracting telescope to study the heavens. James Gregory worked out the principle of the reflecting telescope in 1663. About five years later SIR ISAAC NEWTON built a reflecting telescope.

Even small telescopes can bring many interesting sights within the view of an observer. With a small telescope one can see, for example, the craters and seas of the moon, the rings of Saturn, some satellites of Jupiter and Saturn, double stars, clusters, nebulae, and other galaxies.

Some amateur astronomers prefer reflecting telescopes; some prefer refractors. The reflector requires more maintenance and more frequent adjustment, but reflectors are less expensive and usually can be made more easily by amateurs.   C. L. K.

SEE ALSO: ASTRONOMY; LENS, MAN-MADE; LIGHT; MIRROR; OBSERVATORY

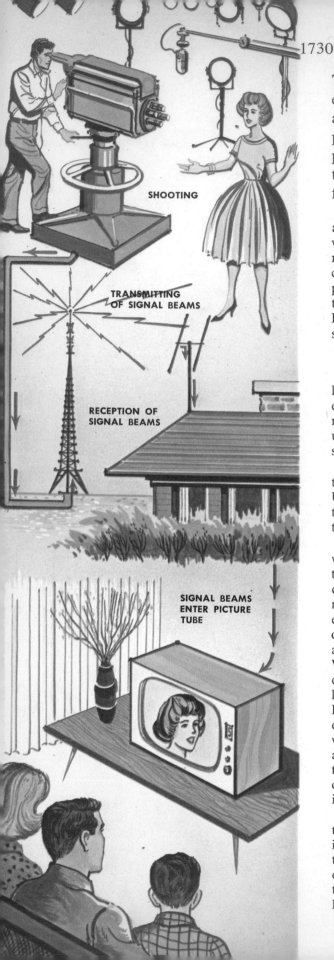

SHOOTING

TRANSMITTING OF SIGNAL BEAMS

RECEPTION OF SIGNAL BEAMS

SIGNAL BEAMS ENTER PICTURE TUBE

Television Television is the system of electronically reproducing visual images. In many respects, the television process is similar to that of the motion picture. In television, however, electron tubes replace the photographic film of the motion picture.

The television process may be described as three principal steps: a scene is recorded with a camera, the images are transmitted on radio waves or special cables, and the receiver converts the electronic images to a picture for viewing. Normally, sound is also transmitted as radio waves with the pictures. However, for certain industrial applications, sound is not required.

TELEVISION CAMERA

The television camera is made up of a lens system, a camera tube, and various electronic circuits. Because these components are so bulky and heavy, the camera is usually mounted on some type of movable stand or tripod.

The lens system focuses the light rays of the scene on the face of the camera tube. Usually, several lenses of varying magnification can be selected and quickly positioned to record closeup or distant objects.

The *image orthicon* tube is the most widely used camera tube because of its extremely high sensitivity and adaptability to changing light conditions. It consists of three main parts: the screen, the target, and the electron gun. When the scene is focused upon the light-sensitive screen, *photoelectrons* are emitted and flow towards the target. When the photoelectrons hit the target, additional electrons are knocked off the target, leaving it with a positive charge at that point. Bright light focused from white objects produces a heavy flow of electrons to the target, while weaker light focused from the dark areas produces a weak flow of electrons. The target, therefore, forms an electronic image of the recorded scene. The entire target image cannot be transmitted all at one time.

The *electron gun* is a device which scans tiny sections of the target very rapidly, sending strong or weak electronic impulses to the transmitter depending upon the strength of the charge on the target. A beam of electrons emitted from the gun moves from the left to right across the target. At the end of

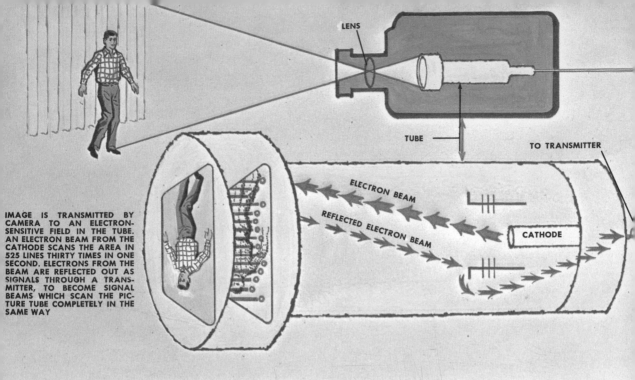

LENS

TUBE

TO TRANSMITTER

ELECTRON BEAM

REFLECTED ELECTRON BEAM

CATHODE

IMAGE IS TRANSMITTED BY CAMERA TO AN ELECTRON-SENSITIVE FIELD IN THE TUBE. AN ELECTRON BEAM FROM THE CATHODE SCANS THE AREA IN 525 LINES THIRTY TIMES IN ONE SECOND. ELECTRONS FROM THE BEAM ARE REFLECTED OUT AS SIGNALS THROUGH A TRANSMITTER, TO BECOME SIGNAL BEAMS WHICH SCAN THE PICTURE TUBE COMPLETELY IN THE SAME WAY

each sweep, the beam returns to the left but moves a fraction of an inch lower.

This process is repeated until the entire picture is scanned from the upper left to the lower right corner. Two separate scans, called *interlace scanning,* are made to cover the whole image. The first, third, fifth, etc., horizontal lines are swept first, then the second, fourth, sixth, etc., lines are swept to complete the picture. Federal Communications Commission regulations require that an image be scanned with 525 lines at the rate of 30 pictures per second. The scanning beam, therefore, moves horizontally in less than 1/15,000 of a second, completing the odd-line scan in 1/60 of a second.

Electrons emitted from the gun are returned to the circuit after striking the target. If the beam hits a highly charged spot (bright area), the positive charge attracts the electrons and fewer electrons are returned. If a low charged spot (dark area) is hit, more electrons are bounced back. These returning electron pulses carry the picture information to the transmitter where they are combined with the signals needed to keep the camera tube and receiver picture tube synchronized (in step).

TELEVISION TRANSMITTER

The transmitter is a special RADIO wave generator which sends the video signals through the air. A high-energy electromagnetic wave (carrier) generated by the transmitter is changed in shape by the addition of the varying video signals. The resulting modulated wave is of very high frequency and can normally be transmitted only as far as the eye can see—approximately 150 miles. To attain maximum reception, television broadcasting and receiver antennas are placed as high as possible.

Microwave towers, placed every 30 miles, receive, amplify, and relay the transmitted signals over long distances by changing them to microwave radio signals. *Coaxial cables,* used for long distance communications by TELEPHONE companies, are employed for nationwide transmission of television signals.

Video signals are transmitted on one of 12 Very High Frequency (VHF) or 70 Ultra High Frequency (UHF) channels.

TELEVISION RECEIVER

The television receiver reverses the process of the transmitter and camera so that a picture can be viewed. An antenna intercepts the weak modulated carrier wave and feeds it to the electronic components of the receiver set. The video signal is amplified and separated from the carrier wave on which it was transmitted. The video signal is then converted to varying electronic impulses just like those that left the camera. These signals are fed to the controls of the receiving *cathode ray tube,* also called the *kinescope* or *picture* tube. The kinescope reverses the action of the image orthicon. The beam from the electron gun of the kinescope scans the fluorescent screen at the same rate as the

1731

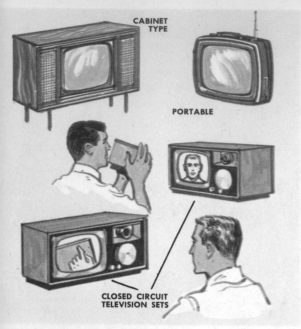

CABINET TYPE

PORTABLE

CLOSED CIRCUIT TELEVISION SETS

camera scanning beam. As the beam of electrons scans the fluorescent face of the screen, light and dark areas made up of tiny dots appear in direct relationship to the intensity of the video signals controlling emission from the gun. Because the scanning rate is so fast and the fluorescent dots continue to glow for a short period of time, persistence of vision makes the whole picture appear to be projected at one time.

COLOR TELEVISION

Thus far, only equipment involving *monochrome,* or black and white, signals has been mentioned. *Color* television is actually transmitted as black and white signals with the following differences. Three image orthicon tubes are required in the television camera, each sensitive to only one color—red, blue, or green. The three different electronic impulses are combined and broadcast as one signal. The color television receiver contains a picture tube with three electron guns, one for each color, and a special phosphor-coated screen. The phosphors are tiny clusters of dots, each cluster containing dots which glow red, blue, or green when excited by their respective electron-beam flow. Because of their closeness, the primary colored dots cannot be seen separately, but appear to blend into the color of the original scene. Color broadcasts can also be seen in black and white since a special black and white signal is required with color transmissions.

CLOSED-CIRCUIT TELEVISION

Anyone with the proper receiver can pick up any broadcast television signal. In closed-circuit television, the signal is directed to a special audience. The signal is not transmitted but sent over special cables directly to the viewers. Although sometimes used to show sports events, the most important uses of closed-circuit television are industrial and educational.

Closed-circuit television systems are used wherever it would be dangerous or difficult for a man to go. For example, the television camera can be placed in a foundry to monitor the pouring of molten metal, on top of a smokestack to monitor industrial waste, or in atomic energy work to monitor the amount of radiation without exposing the operator.

In education, closed-circuit television allows a skilled teacher to perform an experiment before everyone in the school at one time. In medical schools, the television camera can be mounted over an operating table to give all the medical students a close-up of the surgeon's hands and his techniques.

In many closed-circuit television systems a conventional television receiver can be used as the monitor, although the sound is not generally used. Some closed-circuit systems, however, scan with as many as 700 lines. The greater the number of lines scanned, the greater the resolution of the received picture. Special receivers are needed to receive such a picture, however. E. I. D.

SEE ALSO: ANTENNA, CATHODE-RAY TUBE, ELECTRONICS, PERSISTENCE OF VISION, PHOTOELECTRICITY

Tellurium (teh-LOOR-ee-um) Tellurium (element 52) is a scarce element, possessing some metallic properties. In its pure form it is found in igneous rock in Colorado, Bolivia, and Europe. J. F. M. von Reichenstein first isolated tellurium in 1782.

Tellurium (symbol Te) has atomic weight 127.60 (127.61, O = 16). In crystalline form, it is a silvery-white, brittle metal; in its amorphous form, brownish-gray powder.

Gold is chemically inactive but unites readily with tellurium to form gold tellurides, important ores.

Tellurium is used to improve the ductility of steel, as a dye in glass, as an additive in lead alloys, and as catalysts for cracking petroleum. I. K. F.

SEE ALSO: ELEMENTS

Telophase see Mitosis and meiosis

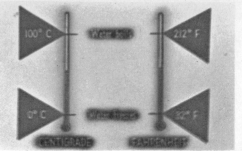

Centigrade and Fahrenheit scales

Temperature (TEM-per-uh-tchoor) One deals with temperature every day. For example, the average person needs to know about the temperature of the air in order to know what to wear and what he can do. The temperature of the air throughout the world varies from about −95° F in Siberia, and even lower in Antarctica, to 135° F in Libya. Air temperature is usually given in the Fahrenheit scale.

Every object holds some heat, down to a temperature called *absolute zero,* which is −273.18°C. or −459.72°F. The theory is that below this temperature molecules cease to move. The temperatures of objects are useful in science to understand the properties of materials and use them better. The scientist relates temperature to the *average kinetic energy* of the molecules of any substance containing *heat* energy.   E. Y. K.

SEE ALSO: ABSOLUTE ZERO, MOLECULAR THEORY

Temperature scales The temperature of different materials can be measured in different scales. Three common temperature scales are used today. They are called the Fahrenheit, Centigrade, and the Absolute or Kelvin. All three scales are based on the freezing and boiling points of water at sea level.

The common household and fever thermometers use the Fahrenheit scale with the freezing point at 32° F and the boiling point at 212° F. Healthy body temperature is between 98.0° and 99.00° Fahrenheit.

The Centigrade scale is used by scientists and in some countries in Europe. On this scale, the FREEZING POINT is 0° C and the BOILING POINT 100° C; therefore, there are 100 divisions between freezing and boiling points of water.

Temperatures in Fahrenheit may be converted to Centigrade temperatures, and vice versa, by using the following formulas:

$$C = 5/9 \ (F - 32)$$
$$F = 9/5 \ C + 32$$

In the Absolute or Kelvin scale, zero degrees is at absolute zero, −273.18° C. There are 100 divisions between the freezing point and boiling point of water, so conversion from the Absolute scale to the Centigrade scale is easy:

$$A = C + 273.15$$
$$C = A - 273.15$$

The Absolute scale has a very important scientific and theoretical use because it can measure extremely cold temperatures. The temperatures at which gases liquify, for example, make it convenient to use the Absolute scale.

An absolute scale based on Fahrenheit, the way Kelvin is based on Centigrade, is sometimes used. It is called the *Rankine* scale. On it water freezes at 491.7°.   E. Y. K.

SEE ALSO: ABSOLUTE ZERO, TEMPERATURE, THERMOMETER

Tempering Tempering is heating steel or iron to a precise temperature, then quickly cooling it to produce a material of greater toughness.

Tendon see Anatomy, Fibrous tissue

Tendon of Achilles The tendon of Achilles is the white, fibrous cord which connects the muscle of the calf of the leg with the heel bone.

Tendril A tendril is a thin, leafless modification of a plant STEM (in the case of the grapevine) or a leaf (in the case of the pea). It attaches to an object, giving the plant support.

Tensile strength Tensile strength is the maximum STRESS a substance can bear without pulling apart. It is measured in pounds per square inch.

Kelvin and Rankine temperature scales

Tentacle (TENN-tuh-kuhl) A tentacle is a whiplike organ for feeling, movement, or defense, found around the head or mouth of some *invertebrates*. It is also a hairlike part of a flower which receives outside stimuli.

SEE: COELENTERATA

Teratology (tair-ah-TAHL-uh-jee) Teratology is the science which studies "monsters," or abnormal formations in animals and plants. Two classes are recognized: (1) malformations—dwarfism, gigantism, absence of limbs; and (2) doubling of bodies, such as Siamese twins.

SEE: EMBRYOLOGY

Terbium (TER-bee-uhm) Terbium is the 65th element, a rare earth. It was discovered in 1842. Today it is purified and separated from the ore by electrolytic methods.

Terbium (symbol Tb) is a silvery-gray metal. It is easily oxidized in the air. The oxide, formula Tb_2O_3, is a white solid, while the peroxide, formula Tb_4O_7, is a dark solid. Nitrate and sulfate salts can also be formed. The atomic weight of terbium is 158.924 (158.93, O = 16). M. S.

Termite Termites, often called *white ants,* are not really ants. They belong to the same insect group as the roaches. There are almost 2000 known species all over the world.

Termites are *social* insects. They live in colonies. The work of the colony is divided up and different jobs are done by different forms of the insect.

Most of the termites in a colony are small and blind with round heads and small jaws. These are the *workers,* both male and female, who do all the feeding and building. They cannot reproduce. The *soldier* termites are also blind and sterile. They are larger than the workers and have huge jaws. Their job is to guard the colony from intruders. The soldiers of some species can spray a repellant fluid.

There is one *king* and one *queen* in each colony. The queen has a greatly enlarged abdomen. She may be four inches long. She does nothing but lay millions of eggs.

The fourth group of adults in the colony are dark, with long filmy wings. In spring, they swarm from the nest, mate, lose their wings and start new colonies.

Each egg laid hatches into a nymph. The nymph may develop into any adult form, depending on the needs of the colony. Its development is thought to depend on hormones secreted by the workers caring for it.

Termites eat anything containing cellulose, principally wood. Their food is predigested by one-celled organisms living in their digestive tracts. They are useful in rain forests because they help return dead trees to humus. But they do millions of dollars of damage to buildings in civilization.

Their homes, made of wood and earth mixed with saliva and excrement, are ingeniously built to provide the proper heat and moisture conditions. E. R. B.

Tern The tern is a slender, swift, graceful bird related to the GULL. It lives near water and eats fish. It has webbed feet for diving, swimming, and fishing. It is black and white, and

A slender black bill and deeply forked tail distinguish roseate terns from other terns

Termite nest

Buchsbaum

✳ THINGS TO DO

MAKING AND STOCKING WOODLAND AND DESERT TERRARIUMS

A WOODLAND TERRARIUM
A glass jar or old aquarium may be used to hold these different earth scenes. To make a woodland terrarium, spread a layer of gravel and bits of charcoal on the bottom; cover this layer with several inches of rich garden soil. Small woodland plants, such as strawberry, fern, and moss may be transplanted into it. Salamanders, toads, and tree frogs enjoy this kind of a world. Do not put the woodland terrarium in direct sunlight, because these plants and animals prefer shady places.

B DESERT TERRARIUM
A desert terrarium needs sandy soil in which cacti and succulent plants are grown. Small snakes and horned toads thrive in this environment. This kind of a terrarium can use more sunlight than the others.

many shades of gray. It grows from nine to twenty-three inches long. Terns form large colonies during the breeding season, and are known to migrate great distances.

The *Aleutian* tern is found on the islands near the coast of Siberia and Alaska and migrates to Japan in the winter.

The *Arctic* tern is found from the Canadian border almost to the North Pole. It migrates to the Antarctic each year, making the round trip of about 22,000 miles in about twenty weeks.

The *black* tern is a plains bird, and is found from Illinois north to Alaska. It may migrate as far as Chile.

Brown's tern is found in California and Mexico during the summer, and as far south as Peru in the winter.

The *common* tern has a black patch on its head, a pearl-gray back and wings, a white, deeply-forked tail, a red bill with a blackish tip, and orange-red feet. It lives from the Gulf States to northern Canada in the summer, and may migrate as far as the southern tip of South America.   M. R. L.

Terramycin see Antibiotics

Terrapin see Turtle

Terrarium (teh-RARE-ee-um) Terrarium means "little world" and is a miniature world built to be like the place in which certain plant or animal life lives. An ant walking around in a woodland terrarium would be as small in comparison as a man walking in a forest. Setting up these little communities helps one to see and understand how plants and animals live together.

✳ **THINGS TO DO**

MAKING AND STOCKING BOG AND SEMI-AQUATIC TERRARIUMS

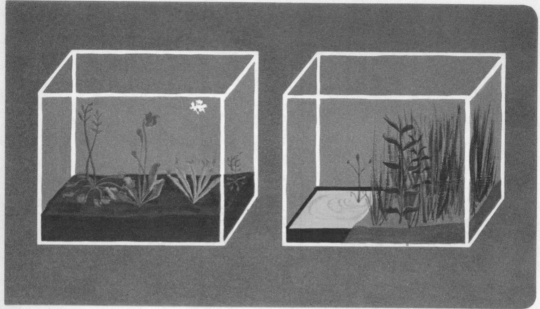

A   BOG TERRARIUM
The bottom of this terrarium should contain a mixture of one part sand, one part peat moss, and one part gravel. Bog life prefers more moisture than the other forms of life. This environment is ideal for insectivorous plants, such as the pitcher plant, sundew, and Venus' flytrap.

B   SEMI-AQUATIC TERRARIUM
The scene in this terrarium is a replica of the environment along a river bank. Place a pan at one end of the container to hold the water; the remaining section should be built up with rich soil. Small plants found on the edge of a stream may be transplanted. Aquatic bladderwort thrives in this world. Tadpoles and water insects may be kept in the water habitat.

Traveling around the country one will observe different *flora* and *fauna* in different environments. Organisms living in the dry, hot desert regions are adapted to the very high temperatures and little water. The plants and animals growing in a bog in the middle of a forest could not survive in a desert, because they need a lower temperature and more water. Before selecting the contents for a terrarium, the relationship of organisms and their environment (ECOLOGY) should be studied. The plants and animals should be placed together in the type of soil and the conditions of moisture best suited for them.   H. J. C.

Tertiary see Cenozoic Era, Geologic time table

Testa see Seed

Testis (TESS-tiss) The testis is the sex gland in the male. Within the testis, sex cells develop or mature into SPERM cells (*spermatozoa*) ready to fertilize egg cells produced by the ovaries of females. In man, maturing of sperm is controlled by *hormones* secreted by the testis and by another gland, the *pituitary,* located below the brain.

The testis consists of many coiled tubes of different widths enclosed in a connective tissue capsule. The outer capsule (*tunica albuginea*) extends partitions (*septa*) into the testis forming compartments around the tubes (*seminiferous tubules*). The tubules contain developing sperm cells and columnar-like cells called sertoli cells.

Mature sperm cells pass from the tubules into less coiled tubes or ducts known as *tubuli recti.* These tubes are lined with *columnar epithelium.*

The tubuli recti connect with still smaller ducts which make up the part of the testis called the *rete testis.* These ducts are lined with *cuboidal* or *squamous* cells bearing *flagella* on their free surfaces.

The rete ducts connect with the *vasa efferentia,* which are ducts lined with clumps of *ciliated* columnar cells alternating with flagellated cuboidal cells.

The vasa efferentia lead to the *epididymis,* a larger coiled tube similar to them in construction. After the sperm pass through all of these ducts, they finally leave the testis through the largest duct, the *vas deferens.*

J. C. K.

SEE ALSO: HISTOLOGY, MITOSIS AND MEIOSIS, REPRODUCTIVE SYSTEMS

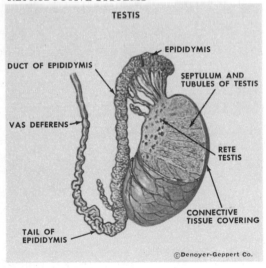

TESTIS

EPIDIDYMIS

DUCT OF EPIDIDYMIS

SEPTULUM AND TUBULES OF TESTIS

VAS DEFERENS

RETE TESTIS

TAIL OF EPIDIDYMIS

CONNECTIVE TISSUE COVERING

©Denoyer-Geppert Co.

Tetanus (TET-ah-nus) Tetanus is a dangerous disease of the nervous system. It is sometimes called *lockjaw.* At the beginning of the disease the muscles of the jaw stiffen and lock.

Tetanus is caused by a poison that a small germ, the *Bacillus tetani,* creates. This germ is *anaerobic,* that is, it lives best where there is no oxygen. Therefore, a deep wound such as that from a nail or a bullet, where air cannot enter easily, is dangerous.

Today, children are given regular injections of tetanus toxoid to build immunity against the disease. A tetanus antitoxin administered after a deep or crushing wound will usually prevent the disease. These injections, plus quick care of wounds by a doctor, make tetanus fairly rare. This is fortunate because the disease can be fatal in untreated cases.

The first symptoms of tetanus are headache, fever, extreme restlessness, and stiffness of the jaw and *esophageal* muscles. Then follow painful spasms of other muscles which, being reflex actions, are aggravated by the slightest noise, air current, or other irritant. The body is often bent backward or to the side. The temperature may rise to as high as 113° F.

The longer it is before symptoms appear, the better the chances for survival. The only treatment for the developed disease is absolute quiet in a dark room, drugs to dull the pain, and liquid nourishment.

Tetanus is easily diagnosed, since only *strychnine poisoning* resembles it. J. M. C.

Textile A textile is a fabric or material made by knitting, weaving, netting, or braiding natural fibers, such as COTTON, WOOL, and SILK or manmade fibers, such as NYLON, rayon, and spun glass.

SEE: SYNTHETIC FABRICS

Thalamus see Brain

Thallium (THAL-ee-um) Thallium is the 81st element. It is a heavy metal with some of the properties of lead. This element has a bluish-white color, and will leave a streak on paper as lead will. Some of its salts are sometimes used as a rat poison. The metal was discovered in 1861 by Sir William Crookes.

Thallium will oxidize easily in the air; and because it is not water soluble, it is usually kept under water to preserve its pure state. Salts, such as the chloride, the nitrate, and the oxide, have uses in organic synthesis, analytical chemistry, and glassmaking.

Thallium (symbol Tl) has atomic weight 204.37 (204.39, O = 16). M. S.

SEE ALSO: ATOM, ELEMENTS

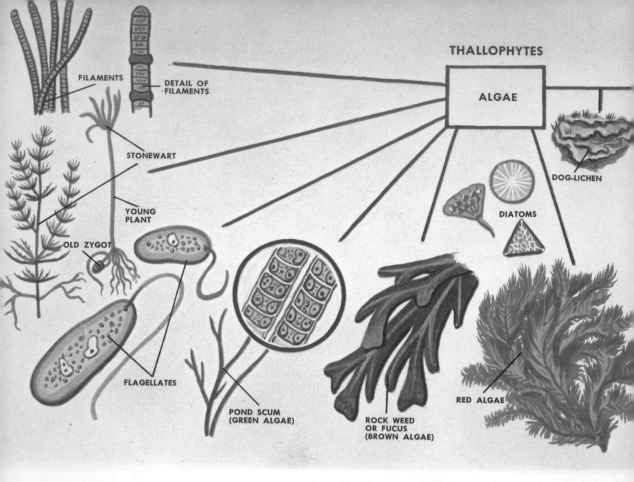

ALGAE

FILAMENTS

DETAIL OF FILAMENTS

STONEWART

DOG-LICHEN

YOUNG PLANT

DIATOMS

OLD ZYGOT

FLAGELLATES

POND SCUM (GREEN ALGAE)

ROCK WEED OR FUCUS (BROWN ALGAE)

RED ALGAE

Thallophytes (THAL-oh-fytes) All the plants in the world, which scientists call the *Plant Kingdom,* can be placed into two large groups. The sub-kingdom *Thallophyta* is the name of a group of very simple plants. The other group is named the subkingdom *Embryophyta* and consists of plants that have many complex parts.

The thallophytes are not like most plants that one can see in a garden or in a forest. They do not have true roots, stems, leaves, flowers, fruits, or seeds. They do not have a vascular system, which is a network of tubes and vessels which carry raw materials to the cells that manufacture the food and then bring the food back to other cells in the plant. Indeed, thallophytes have very simple bodies; food and wastes can be moved directly between cells because they are so close to one another.

Most of these simple plants live in water, which helps them to obtain their food and is necessary for them to reproduce. The male sperm cells must travel through water to reach the female egg cells to start a new plant. The thallophytes live in more varied places than any other plants. They can be found in the ice at the North Pole, in hot springs, on trees, under the ground, far out in the atmosphere, and within many living organisms.

The plants in the subkingdom Thallophyta are further divided into three groups —*algae, fungi,* and *lichens.*

ALGAE

All algae contain CHLOROPHYLL, a green chemical compound which uses light to make food for the plant by the process of PHOTOSYNTHESIS. Algae vary in size from the microscopic *Protococcus* cells growing on the bark of trees to the giant *kelps* in the ocean which reach lengths of 200 feet. Algae may live as a single cell; in long filaments; in round colonies shaped like a ball; or in bulblike forms. Some have plant bodies with leaflike parts, but these are not true LEAVES.

Algae are important in making the soil fertile; a type of red algae is used in making

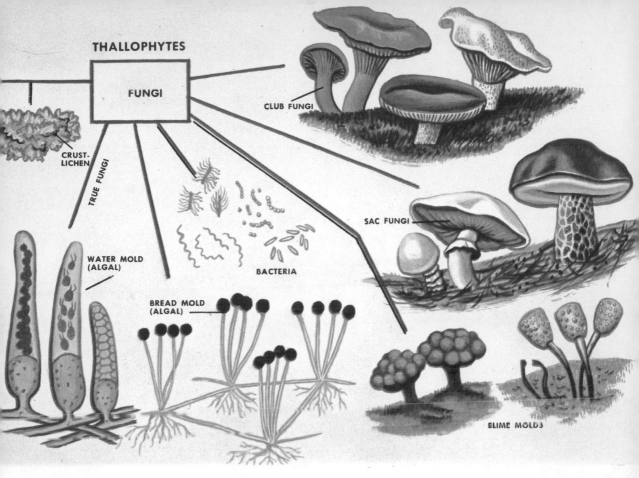

THALLOPHYTES

FUNGI

CRUST-LICHEN

TRUE FUNGI

CLUB FUNGI

SAC FUNGI

WATER MOLD (ALGAL)

BACTERIA

BREAD MOLD (ALGAL)

SLIME MOLDS

agar-agar, a gelatinous material; one kind of red algae known as *Irish moss* is edible; some algae is dried for soups. Certain kinds are dried and powdered for use in baked goods and soups.

FUNGI

Fungi lack chlorophyll and, therefore, cannot manufacture their own food. They are dependent upon external food sources. Plants that live inside or upon other living organisms are called PARASITES. Plants that obtain their food supply from dead or decaying plant or animal materials are called SAPROPHYTES. In this group are found the smallest plants in the world—BACTERIA. Some bacteria cause diseases in plants and animals, for example, pneumonia, tuberculosis, or scarlet fever; but many of them are extremely beneficial to man. They are useful in the production of dairy products, such as cheese or sour cream from milk; in vinegar making; in the preparation of natural sponges; in retting flax; in making wood alcohol, aging meat, purifying sewage, tanning leather, and decaying dead organisms.

Other useful fungi include edible mushrooms, puffballs, and morels. From certain molds *penicillin, streptomycin,* and *neomy-*cin, the wonder drugs of modern medicine, are extracted. YEAST is used in bread-making and in wine fermentation.

Harmful fungi are the molds, rusts, mildews, blights, and blisters that destroy crops, forests, and animal life. Several fungi must alternate their hosts in order to complete their life cycle. For example, wheat RUST lives on the leaves and stems of the wheat plant for several stages of growth, then must find a barberry bush for the last two stages of its life. The blister fungi alternate between the white pine and the gooseberry bush.

LICHENS

Lichens are combinations of algae and fungi. These two different kinds of plants live together in a cooperative partnership called *mutualism,* a kind of *symbiosis.* The algae manufacture food for the plant while the fungi anchor the plant body to rocks or trees and secure raw materials. Lichen is sometimes called *reindeer moss* since it is the only vegetation that grows so close to the North Pole. Some lichens produce blue, brown, and yellow dyes. One is used to make litmus paper, a material used in chemistry to determine acidity or alkalinity.   B. B. G.

SEE ALSO: PLANTS, CLASSIFICATION OF

Thaw Thaw means to become changed from the frozen state to the unfrozen state. It is commonly used to refer to ice and snow which melt (become fluid) when heated.

SEE: MELTING POINT

Theine see Tea

Theory A theory is an attempt to explain certain observed facts or phenomena by reasoning that they are results of other phenomena. A successful theory explains many known facts and suggests where to look for new ones.

SEE: SCIENTIFIC METHOD

Theory of relativity see Einstein, Albert; Relativity

Therapy (THER-ah-pe) Therapy is the treatment of disease. The word therapy comes from the Greek word *therapeia* which means "to heal."

Thermal Thermal is the name given to rising currents of warm air which are almost always present to some degree in the ATMOSPHERE. Glider and sailplane pilots have learned to take advantage of thermals for what is called *soaring* flight.

SEE: AIRPLANE, WEATHER

Thermal unit see British Thermal Unit, Calorie, Heat

Thermite see Bombs

Thermochemistry Thermochemistry is the branch of physical CHEMISTRY which deals with the heat effects accompanying a chemical reaction, the nature and course of the reaction.

The engineer who is concerned with problems of heating, refrigeration, and control of chemical reactions at suitable temperatures needs to know the magnitude of such heat effects. The theoretical scientist also needs such heat data to calculate certain thermodynamic properties of substances.

Modern thermochemical results are usually reported in terms of the *calorie* rather than in terms of the joule. The calorie is scientifically defined as the amount of heat needed to raise the temperature of one gram of water one degree centigrade. The calorie is related to the amount of mechanical work to which it is equivalent: one calorie of heat equals 4.184 absolute joules of mechanical work.

When a change in state occurs, the heat effects accompanying this change are measured in a calorimeter. The CALORIMETER is a reaction vessel immersed in a tank of water, and isolated from its surroundings. The rise in temperature of the water is measured with a sensitive thermometer. The product of the rise in temperature and the total heat capacity of the water and calorimeter tank is a measure of the heat evolved.

Thermochemical data usually are expressed as follows:

$$C + O_2 = CO_2 + 94,000 \text{ calories}$$
$$\text{solid} \quad \text{gas} \quad \text{gas}$$

When one mole (12.01 grams) of solid carbon and one mole (32.00 grams) of gaseous oxygen combine to form one mole (44.01 grams) of gaseous carbon dioxide at constant pressure, 94,000 calories of heat are given off.   D. L. D.

SEE ALSO: HEAT OF FUSION, HEAT OF REACTION, HEAT OF VAPORIZATION

Thermocouple (THER-moh-cuh-puhl) A thermocouple is a device having two junctions, which generates a voltage when the junctions are at dif-

A sensitive ammeter will measure the current produced when the thermocouple (an iron wire and a copper wire) is heated in a flame

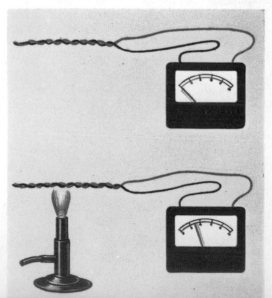

ferent temperatures. Simple thermocouples can be made by joining any two dissimilar metals, such as iron and copper, at each end. If the two junctions are kept at differing temperatures, a voltage is created, producing a current in the wires between the junctions.

The German scientist, Thomas Seebeck, discovered this thermoelectric effect in 1821 while studying Volta's theory of contact potential between unlike metals. VOLTA knew that this contact effect was much like the voltage produced by a cell using two metals as electrodes; he saw that this potential changed as temperature changed. Seebeck found the voltage change depended only on the temperature of one metal junction, if the other junction were kept at constant temperature. The voltage produced depended on the particular metals used.

The voltage produced by a single thermocouple, even with temperature differences of a hundred degrees, is only a fractional volt. Still, thermocouples are compact instruments. They have many uses.

THERMOPILES

A thermopile uses several thermocouples connected in series to give higher voltages. It is used as a radiation THERMOMETER and high-temperature *pyrometer*. Temperatures inside furnaces are so high that they would melt ordinary mercury-in-glass thermometers. But these temperatures can be found if the radiant heat emitted from the furnace is measured. This can be done by allowing the radiant heat to fall on a thermopile and then measuring the voltage.

As a remote detector, the radiation thermopile is positioned at the focus of a mirror. Astronomers measure the surface temperature of planets by this method, using their telescope mirrors to focus the heat radiation onto one side of a thermopile.

THERMOCOUPLE METERS

Certain alternating currents cannot be measured accurately by an AMMETER. Thermocouple meters are used in which the unknown current heats a wire coil. The heat of this coil is then detected by a junction. The resulting voltage produces a direct current measured by an ammeter.　D. A. B.

SEE ALSO: THERMOELECTRICITY, VOLTMETER

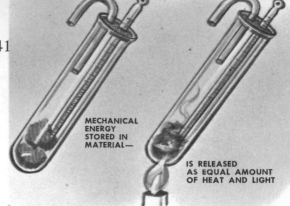

MECHANICAL ENERGY STORED IN MATERIAL—

IS RELEASED AS EQUAL AMOUNT OF HEAT AND LIGHT

The first law of thermodynamics

Thermodynamics Thermodynamics states that energy cannot be destroyed, that energy in other forms tends to be converted to heat energy, and that a pure crystal at absolute zero would have a completely ordered arrangement of atoms.

Thermodynamics is based upon two important relations that have been observed in the interconversion of heat and mechanical, electrical, or other forms of energy. These relations are known as the first and second laws of thermodynamics.

The first law of thermodynamics is also called the *Law of Conservation of Energy*. It may be expressed in several ways: (1) energy may change its form, but it cannot be created or destroyed; (2) when work is transformed into heat, or heat into work, the quantity of work is mechanically equivalent to the quantity of heat; (3) the HEAT entering a system is equal to the increase in energy of the system plus the external work done by the system during the entry.

Heat and motion are both forms of energy. When hot gases in an automobile cylinder push the piston, the gases become cooler. Heat energy is lost, but an equal amount of energy of motion takes place. When objects are rubbed together, energy of motion is lost; but equal heat energy takes its place.

The second law of thermodynamics is often called the *Law of Degradation of Energy*. This law is based on the observation that it is impossible to completely convert a given amount of heat energy into an exact amount of another kind. The reverse process, however, can be carried out. Heat cannot be completely converted to work because some of the work produced is immediately turned back into heat due to friction. To reduce friction, the conversion could be made infinitely slowly. But an infinitely slow

IN TRANSFORMING ENERGY, SOME ENERGY IS ALWAYS LOST AS HEAT AND FRICTION

The second law of thermodynamics

process would require an infinitely long time and therefore would not correspond to any real process.

Since other forms of energy tend to be converted into heat, any system tends to change spontaneously so that this conversion to heat occurs. Also, since the system cannot be put back into its original state except by using extra energy, heat is a more *degraded* form of energy than other forms.

The molecular theory of heat states that heat is the motion, or vibration, of the molecules of a substance. The greater the heat of a substance, the greater the motion of the molecules. This molecular motion is disordered and random. The degraded nature of heat is due to this randomness.

To obtain a measure of the randomness of a system, a quantity called *entropy* is used. To obtain a definition that holds for the ideal case (no FRICTION), as well as for the real case with friction, entropy is defined for an ideal system. When an ideal system at absolute temperature T slowly absorbs a very small amount of heat $\triangle Q$, the entropy of the system increases by the amount $\triangle S$, so that:

$$\triangle S = \frac{\triangle Q}{T}$$

This is the mathematical expression of the second law. For a real system, the increase in entropy is always greater than that for an ideal system.

The second law gives the increase in entropy during a process but it does not give the entropy before the process began. To do this, the third law of thermodynamics is needed. It states that at absolute zero, the entropy of a pure crystal having a perfectly ordered arrangement of molecules would be zero. From the second and third laws, the actual entropy of a substance at any temperature can be calculated. H. W. M.
SEE ALSO: AUTOMOBILE, ENERGY, ENGINE, MOLECULAR THEORY, MOTION

Thermoelectricity That branch of physics which deals with the way in which heat and electrical energy can be directly interconverted is called thermoelectricity. One device that can produce such a direct interconversion is a THERMOCOUPLE.

In homes there are many examples of the *indirect* changing of electricity to heat. When an electric current flows through any conductor, it meets some resistance; and thus some heat is produced, as in an electric iron or toaster. In fact, heat is even produced in the power transmission lines and house wiring, much as heat is produced by mechanical FRICTION. Thus some usable electric energy is lost as unneeded heat. The reverse type of indirect conversion occurs at the power station. There, coal is burned in order to heat water and make steam that turns the turbines; and the turbines drive the electric generators. In this way, heat is indirectly changed into electric energy, since it must first be turned into the mechanical energy of the turbine driving the electric generator.

By contrast, a true thermoelectric device, for example the thermocouple, works directly. It consists of two wires of different metals with their ends joined to form two junctions. In 1821 Thomas Seebeck, experimenting with such junctions, found that if the junction were either heated or cooled a voltage was generated and current flowed through the circuit. Now, thermocouples have important uses. One such use is as a THERMOMETER to measure temperature in inaccessible places. Other uses are measuring alternating currents, and measuring the amount of gas remaining in a vacuum.

Equally important is the reverse thermoelectric effect which was discovered by JEAN PELTIER in 1834, just thirteen years after Seebeck's original discovery. In the Peltier effect, the thermocouple acts as a heat pump, making one junction hotter and the other cooler than the surrounding air or other medium.

After more than one hundred years, the Peltier effect has led to a new invention: a small, efficient refrigerator working on a thermoelectric principle. D. A. B.
SEE ALSO: ENERGY, THERMODYNAMICS

Thermograph see Thermometer

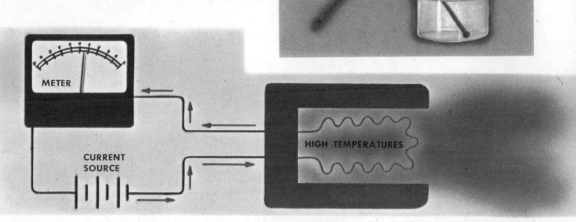

Glass tube thermometers use the principle of expansion of liquids. Liquid rises in the calibrated tube as the thermometer is heated

Courtesy Society For Visual Education, Inc.

METER

CURRENT SOURCE

HIGH TEMPERATURES

Pyrometers are used to measure high temperatures. As the wire becomes hotter, it becomes less able to conduct electric current. A meter measures the current from the wire

Bimetallic thermometers utilize the fact that different metals expand at different rates. Curved strips of two metals, A and B, are fused together. One end is fastened to a scale, the other is connected to a pointer by a spring. Since A expands more than B, the pointer moves to the right as temperature increases

Courtesy Society For Visual Education, Inc.

Thermometer A thermometer is an instrument that tells how hot or how cold a thing is; it measures *temperature*. The temperature of the air outside has an effect on what clothing a person wears. Many foods must be cooled to or cooked at certain temperatures. A furnace must heat at the correct temperature to keep a house warm and comfortable. A thermometer of some kind is used to measure all these temperatures.

Man's early thermometers were rather crude devices. The great GALILEO invented one that measured temperature by the expansion and contraction of air. It was undependable, though modern *Beckman air thermometers* are very exact for measuring small ranges of temperature change. The first *alcohol thermometer* was invented in 1641. Gabriel Daniel Fahrenheit, in 1714, perfected glass-tube thermometers filled with mercury. About thirty years later, Anders Celsius devised the CENTIGRADE scale. In modern times, electric thermometers (THERMOCOUPLES) have been developed.

Thermometers have a great many uses. *Clinical* thermometers are used to measure body temperature. Florists use thermometers so they can keep their greenhouses at the proper temperatures. The measurement of temperature is important in the manufacturing of bricks, china, and glass. An automobile utilizes a thermometer gauge to indicate water temperature. Chemists and physicists rely upon accurate thermometers in their experimentation.

The most common type of thermometer is the glass tube, liquid thermometer. It utilizes the principle of liquid expanding in volume when heated, and contracting in volume when cooled. MERCURY is the liquid element in many household and scientific thermometers. Mercury, because of its high boiling point, is employed for reading high temperatures. Alcohol, with its low freezing point, is the liquid used for reading low temperatures. Many of the wall and outdoor thermometers use alcohol, colored blue or red.

Bimetallic thermometers consist of two metals, such as steel and brass, welded together. Brass expands about twice as fast as steel; therefore, the fused metals bend as the temperature climbs. The *thermograph,* or recording thermometer used by the weather bureau, employs a bimetallic element.

The resistance thermometer and the thermoelectric thermometer are both elec-

✳ THINGS TO DO

MAKING AN AIR THERMOMETER

1. Locate two empty ink bottles or similar containers. Purchase a one-holed stopper for one of the bottles, or make one by drilling a hole in the center of a cork. It will be necessary to put wax around the hole after a piece of glass tubing has been inserted to make the bottle airtight.
2. Fill the second bottle with colored water. Invert the bottle with the stopper over the second bottle, and immerse the end of the glass tube into the solution.
3. Fasten this apparatus to a wooden support.
4. A scale may be calibrated from the readings of a commercial thermometer. When the temperature drops, does the fluid go up or come down in the tube? Does air expand or contract when it gets colder?

tric devices. The platinum thermoelectric thermometer can measure temperatures to 1500° C. High-temperature thermometers are called *pyrometers*.

Temperature is measured in units or degrees. These degrees are not the same on all thermometers. The three most common scales of temperature are the *Fahrenheit, Centigrade,* and *Absolute,* or *Kelvin.* P. F. D.
SEE ALSO: HEAT, TEMPERATURE, TEMPERATURE SCALES, THERMOSTAT

Thermonuclear reaction A thermonuclear reaction occurs when two nuclei of heavy HYDROGEN collide and fuse into a helium-4 nucleus at a high temperature. Tremendous energy is released as nuclear mass is destroyed. In atomic submarines and sea vessels, the high temperatures necessary for continuing thermonuclear reactions and this energy is usefully harnessed.
SEE: NUCLEAR ENERGY

Thermostat A thermostat is an automatic device which regulates temperatures. When a cake is baked in an oven, the thermostat is set for a certain temperature. The oven remains at this same temperature because the thermostat controls the amount of heat entering the oven.

Numerous modern machines and appliances are controlled by the action of thermostats. An automobile's cooling system is regulated by a thermostat which controls the flow of water through the motor. The automobile cigarette lighter is also thermostatically regulated. Home furnaces require a thermostat to keep the temperature at the required number of degrees. Refrigerators, toasters, electric irons, and electric blankets are governed by thermostats. A modern jet airliner requires hundreds of thermostats to help control its complicated engines and instruments.

Thermostats depend upon the expansion and contraction of metals, liquids, or gases. This expansion is used to operate valves or levers or to make or break electrical contacts.

One of the most common thermostats is

The thermostat in a water heater can maintain the temperature of water at the desired level
Courtesy Society For Visual Education, Inc.

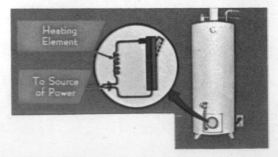

the bimetallic strip thermostat in which two strips of different metals are fused together. These metals expand at different rates when heated. The bimetallic strip bends as it becomes warmer and straightens when cooled. At a certain temperature, the bar closes an electrical contact, making an appliance, furnace, or machine operate. P. F. D.

SEE ALSO: AUTOMATION, HEAT, TEMPERATURE, THERMOMETER

Thigmotropism see Tropism

Thirst Thirst is the sensation which warns that the body needs water. It occurs when the body is losing more water than it is taking in. *Cellular dehydration* in the brain is thought to trigger the thirst sensation.

Helen J. Challand

One of the fifty species of hardy thistle growing wild in North America

Thistle Thistles are a group of plants with spiny, prickly leaves. They grow in any neglected place and spread to gardens, meadows, and grain fields. Plowing, spraying, and burning are methods used to control them.

The Canadian thistle grows to over four feet in height and has silky, fragrant purple flowers. After the blossoms wither, the flower heads form large, downy seed balls which are scattered by the wind. The strong spreading roots start new plants. Goldfinches line their nests with the down of thistles.

The Russian thistle, found in Asia and North America, is a more branching plant with whitish, red or pink flowers. The plant is green in midsummer when other desert plants are brown. P. G. B.

SEE ALSO: WILD FLOWERS

Thorax The thorax is the middle part of an insect's body to which the wings and legs are attached. It is also the part of a vertebrate's trunk, between the neck and the abdomen, containing the heart and lungs.

SEE: INSECTA

Thorium (THOHR-ee-um) Thorium is the 90th element. It is radioactive. Pure thorium is a grayish-white lustrous metal, and can be molded and drawn into fine wires. Thorium and tungsten are in filament wires in light bulbs. It was discovered by Berzelius in 1828.

Thorium can be attacked by concentrated acids, and forms the oxide upon being heated in the air. Salts, such as formate, nitrate, and oxide, are used in medicine. Thorium, with mass number 232, is used in nuclear reactors along with uranium, with mass number 235. The chemical symbol is Th. M. S.

SEE ALSO: ELEMENTS

Thorn A thorn is a woody spine that is sharply pointed. Thorns usually grow out of the bud of a plant. They are nearly always modified, leafless branches.

Some hawthorns with thorns as long as three inches, are planted as living fences. Honey locust trees have long, branching, true thorns. Blackberry and raspberry (bramble) bushes and some rose bushes do not have true thorns, but prickles, growths from the outer layer of a stem. M. R. L.

Thorn apple see Hawthorne

True thorns usually arise from the axil of a leaf, or slightly above it

Brown thrasher

Thrasher The thrashers resemble the thrushes but are larger. They are related to the catbird and mockingbird. They are fine singers and do some imitating of other birds. They are around 11 inches long, have long tails, and down-curved bills. They live near the ground, digging into it for insects.

The *brown thrasher* lives in the United States east of the Rockies. Its back is a chestnut-brown and it has heavy streaks on its light breast. Its lined stick nest is hidden low in a tree or bush, but it sings from the top of a tree or bush. The female lays four or five white or greenish-white, spotted eggs. There are several western thrashers, including the *California thrasher,* the *sage thrasher,* and *Leconte's thrasher* which differ slightly in having grayer backs or browner underparts. All have long curved beaks, and hold their tails up at an angle as they run. E. R. B.

Threadworm see Nemathelminthes, Pinworm, Worms

Thrombin see Blood

Thromboplastin see Blood

Thrombosis (thrahm-BOH-siss) Thrombosis is a condition in which a blood clot is formed within a blood vessel or in the heart. The blood clot is called a *thrombus.* When this occurs in the coronary artery, it is a *coronary thrombosis.* A clot may occur when there is a change in the inner coat of a blood vessel. Such a change may be the result of inflammation, tissue injury, or aging.

In order for a blood clot to form, a substance, *fibrin,* must be present. Fibrin is not normally present in the blood. It is the end product of several chemical reactions. Before fibrin is formed, *thrombin* must be present. Thrombin arises by the interaction of *prothrombin, thromboplastin,* and *calcium.* Thrombin interacts with *fibrinogen* to form fibrin. Under the microscope fibrin resembles a threadlike mesh. Blood cells in the blood vessels are trapped in these meshes.

A blood clot may leave the site of its formation, travel through the blood stream, and eventually lodge in a smaller blood vessel. Such blocking of a vessel by a traveling clot is called *embolism.* Those tissues which are dependent on nourishment by the clogged blood vessels undergo degeneration as a result of the stoppage of the blood flow to them. G. A. D.

SEE ALSO: BLOOD, CIRCULATORY SYSTEMS

Thrush There are several hundred species of thrush found throughout the world. The common characteristics of these birds are the small, slender bills, strong legs on which they hop, and spotted breasts. The robin and bluebird are thrushes. The spotted breasts of the young show their relationship.

The *grayish thrush* is abundant in the orchards of middle America. It is similar to the robin except for its tan breast. The *wood thrush, veery, hermit, olive-backed* and *gray-checked thrushes* are a group of shy forest thrushes that breed in North America and winter in South America. They are about eight inches long, have reddish or greenish-brown backs, and heavily spotted breasts. They eat mostly insects and some worms, spiders and fruit. Their nests are on the ground or in low trees; their eggs are greenish-blues. E. R. B.

Thrust see Aerodynamics

Wood thrush

Thulium (THU-lih-um) Thulium, element number 69, is a scarce metallic element in the rare earth group. Compounds of thulium have a characteristic pale green color. It was discovered by P. T. Cleve in 1879.

In nature, thulium (symbol Tm) is found in combination with other rare-earths in minerals such as gadolinite and euxenite. It has very little commercial value except for its stable isotope Tm^{169}. This isotope, when irradiated in a nuclear reactor, forms Tm^{170}, which can be used as a radiation source for portable X-ray equipment as it gives off X-rays. It has atomic weight 168.934 (168.94, O = 16). I. K. F.

SEE ALSO: ATOM, ELEMENTS, ISOTOPE

Thunder Thunder is produced by violent expansion of air, which is caused by the tremendous heat of lightning.

Light waves travel about 186,000 miles per second, while sound waves travel about 1100 feet per second. Therefore, the sound of thunder is heard after the flash of LIGHTNING is seen.

At times lightning may occur behind a cloud so that the cloud is illuminated. This is called *sheet lightning*. Often lightning is too far away to hear thunder. It is just a muffled roar. V. V. N.

Thundercloud see Weather

Thunderstorm Thunderstorms are local, small-area storms generated by cumulo-nimbus clouds (black, piled-up clouds). Lightning, thunder, heavy rain, and strong gusts of wind are parts of a thunderstorm.

Thunderstorms are characterized by strong upward currents of moist air and the formation of hugh cumulo-nimbus clouds. The atmospheric disturbances usually are associated with high temperatures at the earth's surface and moist air.

These storms are prevalent in certain tropical regions, in the warm season of the intermediate zones, and the warmer hours of the day. The heavy rain, usually of short duration, is a direct result of rapid condensation of water vapor caused by the strong vertical convection currents within the thunderstorm.

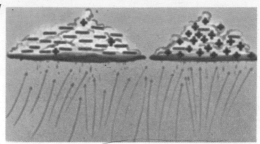
The upward motion of the air against raindrops causes clouds to become charged with static electricity

Photos Courtesy Society For Visual Education, Inc.

Earth acquires the opposite charge. A sudden discharge from negative to positive results in lightning

Clouds form as warm moist air meets a cold front

There are two types of thunderstorms. *Local heat thunderstorms* may occur without warning, due to local CONVECTION (sinking cool air and rising warm air). Rising air currents cause the formation of towering cumulus clouds. These grow to a cumulo-nimbus, which may result in a thunderstorm.

The second type is called the *cold-front thunderstorm*. It is often extensive and more severe than the local heat variety. This kind of thunderstorm occurs along the wind-shift lines of well-developed lows during the warm months. The wind-shift line marks the abrupt meeting place of warm and cold air masses. For example, the warm air mass, which in central and eastern United States often comes from the Gulf of Mexico, may carry large amounts of water vapor. As it is suddenly uplifted by the advancing, underrunning cold front of the polar air mass, dark cumulo-nimbus clouds may form. The thunderstorm that results may be violent and may carry hail. V. V. N.

SEE ALSO: PRECIPITATION, WEATHER, WEATHER FORECASTING

Thyme, an herb

Thyme (TYME) Thyme is a low, shrubby herb with narrow, tiny leaves on short, hairy stems. It has a bitter, fragrant odor when crushed. In cooking, it is used to flavor soups and dressings.

In drug making, *oil-of-thyme* extract gives flavor to dental preparations. The pure oil, *thymol,* is extracted by steam distillation. The oil was formerly used as a drug to treat hookworm. The plant came from the Mediterranean region where it still grows in a natural state. Ancient people used it as an incense and in cooking.   D. A. B.

Thymus (THY-muhs) In humans the thymus is a pink gland that lies between the lungs and near the heart. From birth to two years of age the thymus is large. After that it becomes slightly smaller until in adults the thymus can hardly be recognized. There is growing evidence this gland is important to disease immunity.

Location of the thymus

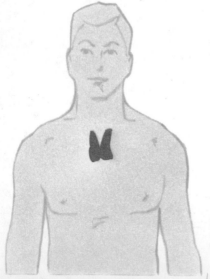

In fish the thymus is above and on both sides of the gill arches. In amphibians it is found near the jaw hinges; in reptiles it is found along the carotid artery that supplies the head. The thymus of crocodiles and birds extends all along the neck close to the esophagus.

The thymus is a ductless gland, a gland whose secretions are distributed by blood or lymph. Each of the two lobes of this gland is divided up and each of the small divisions has a *cortical* or outer part and a *medulla,* or inner part. The cortex resembles a lymphatic gland in structure. In the medulla the lymphoid cells are fewer, and there, groups of epithelial cells are found (the concentric corpuscles of Hassal). The blood supply comes from all the blood vessels in the neighborhood. The nerves supplying the thymus are small and few.   E. M. S.

SEE ALSO: ENDOCRINE GLANDS, GLANDULAR TISSUE

Thyroid The thyroid is a small gland in the neck below the voice box. A large thyroid which appears as a swelling at the base of the throat is called a simple goiter. The most common kind of goiter is caused by too little iodine in the food.

Near the sea coasts the soil and water contain enough iodine, but far inland, glacial soils lack iodine so that foods grown there contain too little of this element for healthy thyroid growth. Today iodides are added to food salts to prevent simple goiter.

Another and more severe thyroid deficiency in children results in *cretinism,* a condition characterized by dwarfness, puffy skin, and mental retardation. In adults severe deficiency results in *myxedema,* characterized by thick puffy skin, scant dry hair, and mental dullness. Taking thyroid extract helps alleviate these conditions.

Hyperthyroidism, or over-active thyroid, causes nervous excitability, goiter, and protruding eyeballs. Cure is accomplished by removal of part of the thyroid gland by surgery.

The thyroid is an endocrine gland which produces *thyroxin* which regulates general METABOLISM. The rate of production of the thyroid gland is regulated by the *anterior pituitary* gland.

The thyroid gland is deep red, and consists of two lobes joined by a tissue bar, or *isthmus,* stretching across the front of the neck. Each lobe has many microscopic, round, closed sacs filled with a colloid, lined with cuboidal cells, and surrounded with blood vessels and nerves. The thyroid's lymphatic vessels are numerous and large.

The thyroid gland is found in the young lamprey but not in the adult. The shark has a single median thyroid; other fish have a pair. Amphibians have a thyroid that consists of numerous amounts of gland tissue close to the end of the membrane around the heart. In reptiles the thyroid is found close to the windpipe, and in birds the gland is paired and close to the arteries supplying the head. A thyroid with lateral lobes is found in all mammals. E. M. S.

SEE ALSO: CRETIN, ENDOCRINE GLANDS, EPITHELIAL TISSUE, PITUITARY GLAND

Thyroxin (thy-RAHK-sihn) see Thyroid

Tibia see Skeleton

Location and enlargement of the thyroid

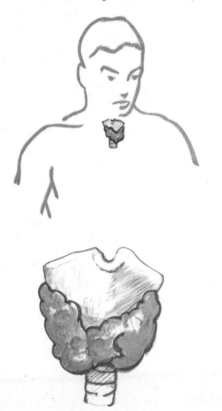

American dog tick

Tick A tick is a tiny animal that attaches itself to man, birds and other animals. It lives by sucking their blood. This PARASITE is no bigger than the tip of a nail. It swells up to the size of a thumb as it fills with blood. Ticks can carry Rocky Mountain spotted fever or Texas fever from infected animals to humans.

The head, thorax, and abdomen are fused, forming a continuous body. A small part of the head region is hinged to the body to give a movable base to the mouthparts. The tick clings to its host with its strong mouthparts. Larvae have six legs and adults have eight. The tick is an *arachnid*.

Ticks can move to people from dogs or other animals or from grasses and shrubs. Eggs are laid on the ground by thousands. The larvae climb into grass and brush off onto animals. A tick must be pulled out gently or its sucking mouthparts may be left in the host and disease may spread. Alcohol, gasoline or a match will free the head. C. L. K.

SEE ALSO: ARACHNIDA, METAMORPHOSIS

Tick fever see Animal diseases

Tidal wave A tidal wave has nothing to do with tides. It is actually a wave which comes from a disturbance in the ocean floor, such as an EARTHQUAKE or a VOLCANO. Sometimes a wave from a great storm is called a tidal wave. The often-used Japanese word for this kind of wave is *tsunami*.

In angry seas, a tidal wave is not easily detected, for a ship rises smoothly toward its crest. When it rushes upon land, the crest may become high and powerful. Then a tidal wave may rise over seventy-five feet high. Crests may be a few hundred miles apart. D. J. I.

SEE ALSO: WAVE

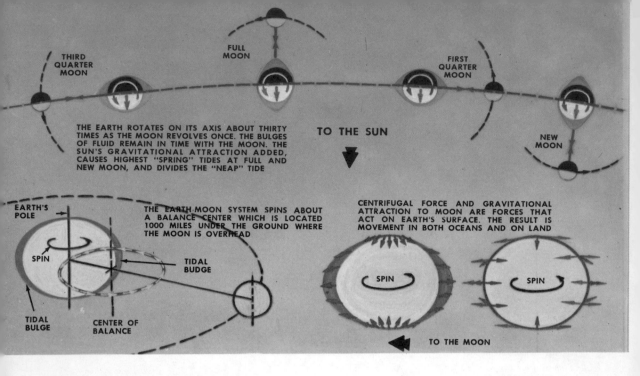

THIRD QUARTER MOON

FULL MOON

FIRST QUARTER MOON

TO THE SUN

NEW MOON

THE EARTH ROTATES ON ITS AXIS ABOUT THIRTY TIMES AS THE MOON REVOLVES ONCE. THE BULGES OF FLUID REMAIN IN TIME WITH THE MOON. THE SUN'S GRAVITATIONAL ATTRACTION ADDED, CAUSES HIGHEST "SPRING" TIDES AT FULL AND NEW MOON, AND DIVIDES THE "NEAP" TIDE

EARTH'S POLE

SPIN

TIDAL BUDGE

TIDAL BULGE

CENTER OF BALANCE

THE EARTH-MOON SYSTEM SPINS ABOUT A BALANCE CENTER WHICH IS LOCATED 1000 MILES UNDER THE GROUND WHERE THE MOON IS OVERHEAD

CENTRIFUGAL FORCE AND GRAVITATIONAL ATTRACTION TO MOON ARE FORCES THAT ACT ON EARTH'S SURFACE. THE RESULT IS MOVEMENT IN BOTH OCEANS AND ON LAND

SPIN

SPIN

TO THE MOON

Tide Twice every day the waters of the ocean rise along the islands and continents of the earth. Twice they sink again, exposing long stretches of wet sand, rocks, and mud. This rise and fall is called the tide. The tide greatly affects water currents, creates and destroys beaches, makes problems for sailing vessels, and affects the breeding habits of many kinds of animals which live in the tidal zones.

Tides are not uniform everywhere. In some parts of the world, there is only one tide daily, as in the Gulf of Mexico. Furthermore, the height of the tides varies from one or two feet at Tahiti and Hawaii, to over fifty feet in the Bay of Fundy. In other places there are two high tides and only one low, while elsewhere only one high tide separates two lows. A rising tide is said to be *flowing* and a falling one, *ebbing*.

Causes of tides are numerous and still incompletely analyzed. The chief causes are the MOON and sun. Since the moon is much closer to the earth than the sun, its gravitational pull is more than twice as great as the sun's, although the sun's mass is 27 million times as large! On one side of the globe, the sun or moon, or both, pulls the water toward itself. Because the ground surface of the earth is also pulled, its opposite side is slightly flattened, causing the water to rise from *inertia* so that high tide

occurs simultaneously on opposite sides, or *antipodes,* of the earth. The same thing happens when a person is suddenly pulled to one side by one arm. The other arm tends to fly outward and away from the direction of the pull.

When the moon is either full or new, the sun and moon are in a straight line with the earth. Their combined force raises the ocean to its maximum high levels, called *spring tides*. However, when the moon is at an angle from the line from Earth to sun during its first and third quarters, it pulls against the sun. High tides, called *neaps,* do not then run so high.

Another factor causing tides is *oscillation.* Just as a large pan of water will rock back and forth when it is disturbed, so the OCEAN waters also rock in the basins which they occupy. These basins occur throughout the ocean, some covering thousands of square miles, others much fewer. When the tide and the *period,* or *rhythm,* of oscillation coincide, tides are greatly exaggerated.

The shape of the local basin and shoreline also affect tides. Water forced into a narrow channel will undergo a funneling flow, and thus will rise very high on the sides of the channel. This is true in the Bay of Fundy. On the other hand, the island of Tahiti is situated in a very large, open basin; therefore, tidal rise is slight because it is distributed over a very wide area.

A less familiar, but no less spectacular sight, is a *bore.* A rising tide at the mouth of a river sheltered on the seaward side by

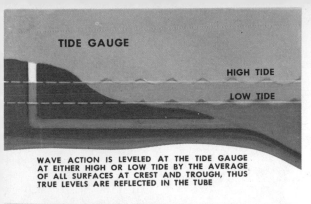

TIDE GAUGE

HIGH TIDE

LOW TIDE

WAVE ACTION IS LEVELED AT THE TIDE GAUGE
AT EITHER HIGH OR LOW TIDE BY THE AVERAGE
OF ALL SURFACES AT CREST AND TROUGH, THUS
TRUE LEVELS ARE REFLECTED IN THE TUBE

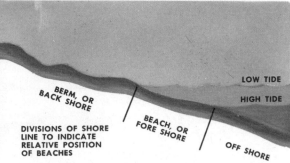

BERM, OR
BACK SHORE

BEACH, OR
FORE SHORE

LOW TIDE

HIGH TIDE

OFF SHORE

DIVISIONS OF SHORE
LINE TO INDICATE
RELATIVE POSITION
OF BEACHES

Low tide exposes a beach below the cliff

a SAND BAR may be held back for a time. As the water gathers offshore from the sand bar, it builds up pressure which finally allows it to spill over the sand bar, sending a wall of water rushing up the stream. The largest and most dangerous bore occurs in the Tsientang River in China where its crest averages nine to ten feet. At spring tide it may run as high as twenty-five feet.

Tides are important in maintaining beaches. The inter-tidal zones are sandy or graveled stretches of shore line which occur between high and low tidal levels. In general, beaches are built up during the summer by deposits of sand laid down by relatively gentle tides and strong on-shore waves. During stormy seasons, usually in winter, the outgoing or off-shore currents are turbulent and swift; and they carry the sand out to sea.

Beach areas are further divided into three zones. The *berm,* or back shore, is the area of dunes and low mounds which is never wetted by the sea. Below that lies the *foreshore,* or beach proper, this area lies between the highest tidal mark and the lowest ebb. Below the lowest ebb is the *offshore* region, entirely under water.

It is common to use the word "tide" in two other ways—"tidal wave" and "riptide." A TIDAL WAVE has nothing to do with the tides. Rather, it is a large crest of water caused by deep volcanic activity, or other crustal shifting. To distinguish it from a true tide, oceanographers call such a crest a *tsunami.* No periodic tides occur in lakes.

But strong, low pressure centers over a large lake cause tidal-wave swells called *seiches.*

The other term, *riptide,* is really a swift, off-shore current produced by a combination of large breakers and shoreline currents, and not directly by the tide.   R. N. J.
SEE ALSO: OCEANOGRAPHY, SEA LEVEL, WAVE

Tiger see Cat family

Tiger lily see Lily

Timber see Economic botany, Forest products, Forestry

Time zones If one were to travel across continents or oceans, one would notice that the time changes in certain places. When traveling from east to west, it is necessary to set a watch back one hour at these certain places. But when traveling from west to east, a watch must be set ahead. These places where time changes are the beginning of new time zones.

Since time changes as the earth spins on its axis from west to east the earth has been divided by man into time zones. Imaginary lines are drawn from the North Pole to the South Pole, much like the dividing sections of a peeled orange. These lines are called lines of *longitude,* or *meridians.*

In 1884, at the Washington Meridian Conference, nations of the world agreed to divide the earth into time zones. These zones were based on lines of longitude or meridians 15 degrees apart. Since 360 divided by 15 equals 24, it is apparent that each time zone marks one hour on a day's time. Approximately one hour passes as the earth rotates for each 15 degrees of its surface. One complete rotation occurs in 24 hours.

The conference also decided that the meridian of the city of Greenwich, England, would be the meridian of 0 degrees longitude. Meridians east of Greenwich up to longitude 180 degrees are called *east* longi-

✳ **THINGS TO DO**

TELLING TIME AROUND THE WORLD

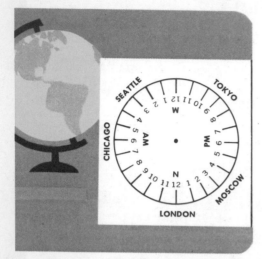

When it is noon in Chicago, what time is it in London or Sydney?

1   Fasten a circle in the center of a large sheet of tagboard with a clip which permits the circle to rotate.

2   Mark off the circle into twenty-four equal parts by bisecting the center. These lines will serve as the longitudes of the earth.

3   Number them consecutively from 12:00 P.M. around to 11:00 A.M. Using a globe find the longitude of a particular city in which you are interested and write it on the corresponding line of your time table.

4   As you work with this instrument you will become very proficient at quickly estimating time around the world.

tude, while all meridians west of Greenwich up to 180 degrees are called *west* longitude.

As an example of time zones, consider Philadelphia, which is 75 degrees west longitude. This is five time meridians west of Greenwich. Therefore, there is a difference of five hours between the clocks of Greenwich and Philadelphia.

"Daylight saving" time is a local adjustment, advancing an hour ahead of the accepted meridian time. This is done to allow an added hour of daylight.   v. v. n.

SEE ALSO: CALENDAR, EARTH, GEOGRAPHY, INTERNATIONAL DATE LINE

Long blades and green flowers of timothy

Timothy Timothy is a tall member of the grass family which is grown as hay for animal feed. In the past it was usually used to feed horses. It is often mixed with red clover for planting. The name of this grass came from the man, Timothy Hanson, who brought it from Europe in the early eighteenth century.

Timothy is commonly found in fields and meadows and along the roadside. It is easily recognized by its pale-green flower parts which are about two to three inches long and look like tiny cattails. The leaves are rather broad and ribbon-shaped. The plants grow to about two feet in height. It is sometimes called "cat-tail" grass.   D. J. I.

SEE ALSO: GRASSES

Tin Tin is a soft, white metallic element. It is highly malleable, which means it can easily be hammered into thin sheets. If a piece of pure tin is bent, it produces a crackling sound. When tin is exposed to low temperatures over a long period, the metal crumbles to a gray powder called *tin pest* or *tin disease.*

The leading ore from which metallic tin is obtained is called *tinstone* or *cassiterite,* formula SnO_2. Most of the world's supply comes from British Malaya, Bolivia, and the Dutch Indies. Tin (symbol Sn from Latin *Stannum*) has atomic number 50 and atomic weight 118.69 (118.70, O = 16).

Since tin ore usually contains many impurities, these must be removed before the metal can be extracted. The ore is roughly pulverized and concentrated by washing and frothing. The ore is then roasted to oxidize impurities such as sulfur and arsenic. Acid-soluble impurities are removed by leaching the ore with acid. The tin oxide is then reduced with carbon:

$$SnO_2 + 2C \rightarrow Sn + 2CO\uparrow$$

As the molten tin, 99.5 per cent pure, flows away from the impurities, it is cast in blocks (block tin).

Tin plate—for the coating of tin cans—is an important product of tin. Thin sheets of iron or copper are dipped into melted tin—a process similar to galvanizing. Tin prevents iron from rusting, but once the tin surface is broken, the iron will rust faster than usual.

Because of its low melting point, tin is a leading component in many ALLOYS, such as Wood's metal, Rose's metal, solder, type metal, Babbitt metal for bearings, bronze, bell metal, and pewter. Due to tin's malleability tin foil was used in the wrapping of candies, gum, and many foodstuffs. The growing scarcity of tin has led to the substitution of aluminum foil, plastics, and papers. Block tin is used in the food industry for moving slightly acidified solutions, such as carbonated beverage syrups. It also is used in water stills.   D. L. D.

SEE ALSO: ELEMENTS, METAL

Tincture A tincture is an ALCOHOL solution of some drug or medicine. It contains a single element such as iodine, or a single compound, or the part of a plant which will dissolve, such as cinchona bark.

SEE: DRUGS

Tintype see Photography

Tissue see Anatomy, Histology

Tissue culture Animals are made of many thousands of cells. Each cell in the body of a frog, a chick, a mouse, or a human has its own work to do to keep itself alive and to keep the whole animal alive. Each cell also depends upon the rest of the body to supply it with food and to carry away waste materials that poison it. For these

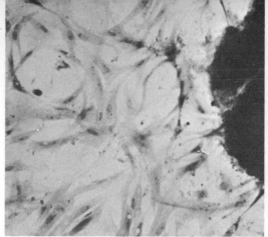

Beatrice Garber

The individual heart fibroblasts (connective tissue cells) can be seen in this magnified view of a culture of heart tissue

reasons, it was believed for many years that cells could not live if they were removed from a living animal.

About 50 years ago, however, it was learned that cells can live outside the animal's body if they are given a proper place to live in; if they are supplied the right food; and if the wastes that form can be removed. Keeping cells alive outside the animal's body is called tissue culture.

In 1907, Ross Harrison removed small pieces of very young *embryonic nerve tissue* from the developing egg of a frog and placed them in hanging drop cultures of clotted lymph taken from an adult frog. He carefully sealed them so that they would not be contaminated with bacteria or mold. He found that the nerve cells not only stayed alive, but grew actively and migrated out into the clotted medium. This experiment was the beginning of the tissue culture technique.

Alexis Carrel, a Nobel Prize winner, improved further the methods of keeping cells alive outside the body. Strains of connective tissue cells originally taken from the heart of a developing chick have been kept alive for over 25 years—certainly many times the normal life span of the chick.

In the early days of tissue culture, the juices extracted from embryonic tissue provided the nutrients, and the clotted plasma of adult chicken blood was the preferred growth medium. Strict aseptic conditions were necessary so that bacteria and fungi would not invade the cultures. Today, after years of experience, it has become simpler and more successful to use synthetic materials for a culture medium and antibiotics to control bacteria and fungi.

It is advantageous to isolate cells in a tissue culture to study what these cells can do when they are not under the influence of the rest of the body. It is also possible to watch cells in a tissue culture under the microscope in a living condition. Moving pictures can be taken of their activities. Various kinds of cells have been studied alone in tissue culture: for example, nerve cells, heart cells, kidney cells, cancer cells. By watching these cells grow, it is possible to study how they develop, what makes them assume certain shapes, and what relationships exist between various cells.   B. B. G.
SEE ALSO: HISTOLOGY

Titanium (tye-TAY-nee-um) Titanium, atomic number 22, is a silver colored metal discovered in 1791. Although the ores are abundant it is difficult and costly to extract titanium.

Titanium is used a great deal in combination with other metals in alloys. It contributes greater strength to the alloys and makes them more resistant to corrosion.

Titanium (symbol Ti) has atomic weight 47.90 (unchanged for carbon).   M. S.
SEE ALSO: ATOM, ELEMENTS

Titmouse A titmouse is a small, fluffy bird. It lives in the woods, eating insects and insect eggs and seeds. It moves like an acrobat around a tree hunting for insects in the bark and leaves. Titmice are closely related to chickadees.

Many colorful species live in Europe, Asia and Africa. The *tufted titmouse,* a grayish crested bird with brown spots near its legs, lives in the eastern United States. The *plain titmouse* of the Southwest is similar except for the brown. The *bush tit,* a small brownish-gray bird, lives in flocks in the scrubby plants of the West. Titmice nest in holes, which they stuff with leaves and moss. They lay speckled white eggs.   E. R. B.

Titov, Major Gherman Stepanovich (TEE-tawf) (1935-) Major Titov is the Russian COSMONAUT who, on August 6, 1961, circled the globe seventeen times, making a 434,000 mile flight in his five-ton spaceship "Vostok II." He was aloft for twenty-five hours, eighteen minutes. Though Titov manually controlled the return of his spaceship, he himself landed by parachute not far from his ship.

It is interesting to note that until the fall of 1962 Gherman Titov, Colonel John Glenn, and Lt. Commander M. Scott Carpenter were the only men ever to see the rising and setting of the sun more than once in twenty-four hours.   D. H. J.
SEE ALSO: SPACE TRAVEL

Titration (tye-TRAY-shun) Titration is one of the ways a chemist tests a solution to find out its strength. He uses, for his titration, a solution whose strength he already knows (a standard solution).

Tufted titmouse, a common forest bird

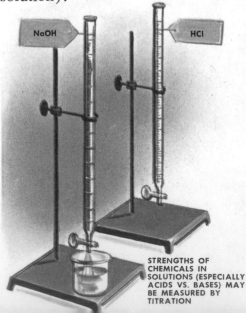

STRENGTHS OF CHEMICALS IN SOLUTIONS (ESPECIALLY ACIDS VS. BASES) MAY BE MEASURED BY TITRATION

In practice, the unknown solution—an acid of unknown strength, for example—is put in a beaker; and the solution of known strength, in this case a base (caustic), is dripped into the beaker from a long tube or *burette*. An indicator, usually a colored organic compound, which has been added to the unknown solution, changes color when just enough base has been added to the solution to neutralize the acid. After the amount of base used in the titration is noted, a calculation can be made to determine the strength of the unknown acid solution. M. S.
SEE ALSO: ACIDS AND BASES, ALKALI

TNT see Explosives

Toad A toad is a small animal that resembles a FROG. It is an amphibian. It spends part of its life on land and part in the water. It usually has a stout, heavy body three or four inches long, a large head, and frog-like eyes. It has strong hind legs which enable it to hop about looking for insects to eat. The toad catches food with its quick, sticky tongue. Its tongue is attached at the front of the mouth. It has a large mouth, but no teeth.

The toad has no tail. Its brownish back is covered with lumps and warts. It is grayish-white underneath and speckled with black spots. This coloring helps the toad to hide from its enemies. The toad has short fore-legs with separate toes. Its long hind legs have partially webbed toes.

The toad lives most of its life on land, except during the spring breeding period. The eggs are laid in the water, several thousand in jelly-like strings. Tadpoles hatch in just a few days. During the next two months, the tadpoles grow larger, the long tail is absorbed into the body, legs appear, and lungs replace the gills. The toad then moves to dry land where it may live as long as thirty years.

The toad hibernates in cold weather. It does some of its breathing and much of its drinking through its skin. It sheds and devours its own skin periodically. It spends much of its time half buried in the dirt. When attacked by an ememy it may puff up its body. Its only efficient means of protection are skin glands which secrete a dis-

Buchsbaum

During the mating season in spring, the shrill call of the male toad to the female can be heard at night near water

The toad's shrill call is made with the aid of an inflatable air sac in its throat

Courtesy Society For Visual Education, Inc.

The toad rolls its long sticky tongue into its mouth when it is not in use

tasteful acid irritant.

Toads differ from frogs in many ways—their hind legs are shorter; their hopping powers are inferior; their skins are dry and warty; their eggs are laid in strings; they live on land most of the time. M. R. L.
SEE ALSO: AMPHIBIAN, METAMORPHOSIS, PROTECTIVE COLORATION

Toadstool Toadstool is a term sometimes applied to poisonous MUSHROOMS — fleshy, umbrella-shaped fungi. It was once believed that toads sat on them.

A well-planned tobacco field in Maryland, with terraces, grassed terrace outlets, and ridged rows, for erosion control and drainage

Tobacco Tobacco is a plant that has been under cultivation for many centuries. The United States leads the world in the production of tobacco. The cured and aged tobacco leaf is used for snuff, chewing tobacco, pipe tobacco, cigarettes, and cigars.

Tobacco was originally an American tropical plant but has been adapted for cultivation in subtropical and temperate regions elsewhere in the world. It is an unbranched annual, growing from three to six feet tall, with large oval leaves.

The tiny tobacco seeds are planted in seed beds, and the seedlings are transplanted when they are four to six inches tall. The best soil is a light, sandy loam, rich in humus and well fertilized. Tobacco requires careful cultivation. When it is fully ripe, as indicated by a change in the color of the leaves, either the whole plant is cut or the leaves alone are harvested.

The freshly harvested leaves are allowed to wilt and then are hung upside down from a framework, in curing barns. Freshly cured leaves must be sorted and aged before using.

M. R. L.

SEE ALSO: NICOTINE

Tomato The tomato is an herb of the nightshade family. The fruit is a *true berry* filled with many small seeds. Man uses the fruit as a vegetable. The perfect flowers have parts divisible by five. The fruits were once called "love apples." The tomato plant is native to Central America.

Tomato plants

The plant looks like a small bush with tiny yellow flowers. As the tomatoes grow heavy, the branches bend to the ground unless they are tied to a stake. The plant should be started in a warm greenhouse and then transplanted to sunny ground. The leaves have a strong scent and are rough to the touch.

The fruit of the tomato plant is usually green until it ripens to a bright red. Some kinds of tomatoes are white or yellow when ripe. There are many varieties of tomato plants developed to grow under different conditions.

P. G. B.

SEE ALSO: VEGETABLE

Tongue (TUNG) The human tongue is a thick, muscular organ in the mouth. TASTE buds, important to the sense of taste, are found on it. The tongue helps in chewing and swallowing food. It is necessary for speech.

All vertebrates have tongues. The tongue of a FROG or a TOAD is sticky. It is attached at the front of the mouth and can be flipped out quickly to catch prey. In fish, the tongue projects up from the floor of the mouth, and is neither muscular nor freely movable. Among snakes, the tongue is probably an organ of smell (olfactory receptor). When inside the mouth, it is retracted into a sheath. The bird tongue lacks well-developed muscles, and is usually covered by horny material.

M. R. L.

SEE ALSO: DIGESTIVE SYSTEM, VOICE

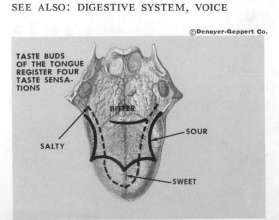

©Denoyer-Geppert Co.

TASTE BUDS OF THE TONGUE REGISTER FOUR TASTE SENSATIONS

BITTER

SALTY

SOUR

SWEET

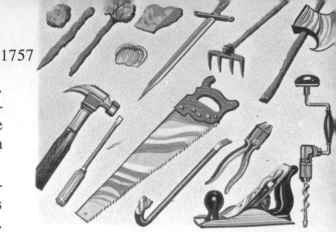

Tonic A tonic is a type of medicine. Tonics are taken to refresh and invigorate the body muscles. Tonics are supposed to help a dull, listless person feel more lively.

Tonsillitis (tahn-suh-LYE-tiss) Tonsillitis is an infection of the tonsils very common in children and adults. The tonsils become red and swollen; swallowing becomes painful. As a rule, the patient has fever and develops a severe pain.

In the past, the tonsils were usually removed as a treatment for repeated tonsillitis. Today, doctors are more conservative, and tonsils are only removed when so large that they interfere with breathing or are the site of abcesses.   G. A. D.

Tonsils Tonsils are lymphatic tissue in the nasal passage and the throat. These glands filter out and destroy bacteria which may have entered the lymph vessels.

Tonsil tissue is divided into three groups: they are the *lingual* tonsils on the back of the tongue, the *pharyngeal* tonsils, or adenoids, in the nasal passage, and the *palatine* tonsils on either side of the soft palate. The palatine tonsils are the largest mass. It is the palatine section that sometimes becomes chronically infected, requiring surgical removal.   J. C. K.

SEE ALSO: LYMPHATIC SYSTEM

Tonus see Muscle system

Location of the palatine tonsils

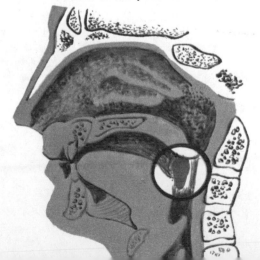

Tools The history of man's development is revealed in the nature of his tools. The very first tools were simple objects of nature. Man's own fists and feet were striking tools. His nails and teeth helped him cut. His hands were tools for holding and shaping. His arms, legs, and jaws could supply leverage for moving.

Sticks and stones, the first tools other than the body, were used in many ways. By lashing a stick to a stone, man made a hammer that was effective for striking. By smoothing and sharpening the edge of a flat stone, a knife was made which had a more durable cutting surface than the jagged edge of a shell or the splinter of hard wood.

Gradually, man also discovered the uses for metals. Thus from the Wood and Stone Age, man progressed into the Bronze Age. He made files and crude tongs during this period. After he discovered iron and ushered in the Iron Age, man developed new tools which were stronger and longer-lasting than those invented earlier. As the variety and quality of tools increased, civilization also developed.

STEEL was an important discovery in the Middle Ages, but was principally used for weapons. During the 1700's, steel tools were made. Later, alloy steel was developed, and led to the manufacture of hard, flexible

HORIZONTAL MILLING MACHINE

PLANING MACHINE

AUTOMATIC GUIDING MACHINE

LARGE RADIAL DRILL

tools that were stronger, sharper, and more durable than any ever known before. Later in the 1700's, tools were designed that could be driven by mechanical power; thus the Machine Age began.

Today there are tools of every imaginable kind. There are striking tools (hammers), cutting tools (saws), shaping tools (lathes), holding tools (vises), leverage tools (crowbars); and there are grinding tools, boring tools, measuring tools, guiding tools, and many special-purpose tools that are used by specialized tradesmen, such as the jeweler, gardener-farmer, bricklayer, and so on.

Many hand tools make use of four of the six simple machines; the *lever,* the *wedge,* the *inclined plane,* and the *screw.* The other two principles of simple machines —the *wheel and axle,* and the *pulley*—are used in complicated machine tools.

HAND TOOLS

While the principles of hand tools have changed little throughout the centuries, the shape of many have changed considerably.

The hammer, with its many variations, is a striking tool. It is also used to crush. The screwdriver is actually a leverage tool, although its main use is to tighten or to loosen screws. Both the hammer and screwdriver are general-purpose tools.

In the cutting and shaping category are the saw, the chisel, and the plane. Saws cut material in many different ways, depending upon the type of saw. The wood chisel chips wooden surfaces if the handle end is hammered. The cold chisel does similar work to metal surfaces. The plane cuts and shapes wood surfaces.

The bit, brace and reamer are drilling and reaming tools. The bit and brace is a standard drilling tool, while the reamer enlarges a hole to a more accurate diameter.

Measuring tools come in many varieties, including the folding rule, the metal tape rule, many gauges, micrometers, calipers, combination squares, and compasses.

MACHINE TOOLS

A machine tool is a power-driven tool that alters the size, shape, or finish of material such as metal, wood, or plastic. A true machine tool does at least four chores. It holds a workpiece, holds a cutting tool, moves one or both of these objects, and provides a feeding movement for the tool or the workpiece. The machine tool performs with exceptional precision and accuracy. It is therefore possible to produce two parts, or thousands of parts, that are identical.

There are over four hundred kinds of machine tools in industry today. They may be very small bench devices or complicated machines weighing hundreds of tons. They perform thousands of operations, and produce tiny nuts as well as huge turbine rotors —both with precision.

While these tools do a multitude of tasks, they perform by using only seven basic principles: *turning, planing, milling, drilling, power-sawing, grinding,* and *metal-working.*

The lathe is a basic tool for the turning operation. By rotating a workpiece against a fixed tool having a single edge, the tool causes a cutting action; and the line of cut forms a cylindrical surface.

In the planing operation, a planer produces a flat surface by its cutting action. This takes place when the workpiece is moved back and forth against the stationary cutting tool. Another tool, a shaper, is smaller than a planer, but planes metal by cutting action opposite to that of the planer. A single-edged tool moves back and forth, and the workpiece is fed into the cutting tool. A broaching machine is most useful for internal cutting.

A milling machine is used to produce a flat, curved, or irregular surface. The milling operation is opposite to that of the lathe, for the milling machine feeds the workpiece against rotating milling cutters.

The drilling operation makes and finishes a special hole. Drill presses make the hole, borers or boring mills enlarge or perfect the hole (reamers also accomplish this task. faster), while a tapping machine threads the inside of the hole.

Power sawing is the quickest method for cutting wood and metal. The band machine, circular saw, and reciprocating saws are common tools in this category.

Grinding removes material by feeding a workpiece against a rotating ABRASIVE. It is really a cutting operation. After the grinder removes the metal, lapping is done to correct minor surface imperfections. Honers are fine grinders used after boring or reaming.

Metal-working operations refer to processes which shape metals by pressure, heat, or both. They also include cutting operations. Shears cut the metal, while press brakes, forming rolls, and roll straighteners bend the metal. Hot forging is done on drop hammers, and hydraulic presses. The punch press, a very versatile machine, can punch a hole in sheet metal; or when fitted with certain dies, it can punch out the metal in relation to the die pattern.   D. L. D.

SEE ALSO: ARCHEOLOGY; EVOLUTION OF MAN; MACHINERY; MACHINES, SIMPLE

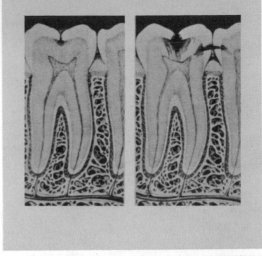

TODAY'S HEALTH, published by AMERICAN MEDICAL ASSOCIATION
In the first stage of decay, the enamel is penetrated. Next, the softer dentine is attacked

Tooth decay Tooth decay, or *dental caries,* is said to be mankind's most common disease. It is caused directly by acid made from sugars and starches, by germs or bacteria that live on the surface of the teeth. The more one eats sugar and starch the more acid is formed in the mouth. The acid then may eat through the enamel of a tooth, causing a *cavity* or hole and then decay. If the cavity is not promptly cleaned out and filled by the dentist, the ivorylike dentine or body of the tooth becomes decayed, and eventually the pulp is exposed.

The pulp is killed and an abscess forms. Finally, the molar is extracted and a nearby bicuspid also becomes abscessed

TODAY'S HEALTH, published by AMERICAN MEDICAL ASSOCIATION

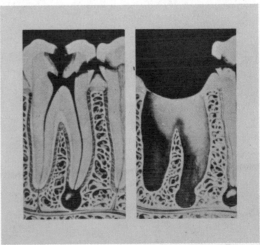

If the exposed pulp is infected, an abscess may occur. An abscess is a pus sac formed at the root-end of the tooth. INFECTION from this spot may be carried throughout the body; so the infected tooth usually must be removed to protect the person's health.

The amount of sugar and starch in the diet does not alone determine the amount of decay that occurs. Some people have teeth which are more resistant or susceptible to decay than others. The condition of the teeth is a factor; a weak condition of the enamel will encourage decay; the acidity of saliva affects decay; and some think a person's emotional state may assist decay.

If food becomes lodged in crevices of a tooth or between teeth and is not removed quickly, these food particles furnish protected breeding places for acid-producing bacteria. The most common decay spots are the spots most difficult to brush—the chewing surfaces of the back teeth, and places where teeth touch each other.

Prevention of tooth decay is still not totally understood. Cutting down on sweets, especially between meals, is recommended to reduce cavities. A healthy, well-balanced diet, regular and proper brushing, and a visit to the dentist at frequent intervals aid in reducing decay. Applying *sodium fluoride* solution to children's teeth (to harden the enamel) helps the teeth resist decay. Some communities now add fluorides to their water supply for this purpose.   D. L. D.

SEE ALSO: TEETH

Topaz (TOH-pazz) Topaz is a valuable GEM (mineral) named after an island in the Red Sea, Topazion, where the gems were once found. Large crystals of blue and white topaz are common all over the world, but yellow topaz is the most valuable because it is the most rare. The finest yellow crystals are found in Brazil.

Uncut natural topaz

J. Daniel Willems

Heat will change yellow topaz to pink. Pink stones are also used in jewelry. Colorless topaz, which has little value, is sometimes cut to imitate diamonds. Quartz may be mistaken for topaz, but true topaz can be distinguished by its greater hardness. Its hardness is 8; its chemical formula, $Al_2SiO_4(FlOH)_2$.   J. M. C.

Topography (tuh-PAHG-ruh-fee) Topography refers to land surface. It is concerned with the manner in which the outer layer of the earth rises in hills, plateaus, and mountains, and sinks in valleys and other depressions. Topography may be concerned with the broader land arrangements of a whole state, nation, or continent, as well as with a small region.

The topography of an area is often charted. Measurements of elevations and depressions, including notations of lake basins and river beds, make up complex data which are used by conservation departments and geological surveys. This data is not only arranged into statistics, but is translated by map-makers into maps which show visually the topographical aspects of a region, usually by the use of several colors, shading techniques, or contour lines. The most graphic representations of this sort are found in the so-called *contour maps* which have physical rises and depressions, that is, actual miniature mountains and valleys constructed on the map surface.   D. J. I.

SEE ALSO: GEOGRAPHY, MAP-MAKING

Topsoil A vertical section through a well-developed soil shows three distinct layers. The fairly loose, porous, usually dark top layer is the *topsoil*. Below this is the lighter more compact layer called the *subsoil*. Below this is the *parent material* from which the subsoil and topsoil is derived.

Topsoil contains sand, silt, and clay and is rich in *humus,* the organic material from decayed plants and animal wastes. Its soluble minerals help plants grow. The bacteria and earthworms in it help fertilize it and keep it porous.   V. V. N.

SEE ALSO: AGRICULTURE, SOIL TYPES

Tornado A tornado is a small-sized but violent storm. It starts when a current of cold air meets a current of warm moist air.

A rapid whirling movement of winds develops around a center of very low pressure. The dark, funnel-shaped tornado cloud travels southwest to northeast at 30 to 40 miles an hour, rising and falling. It causes destruction where it touches the ground. Tornadoes occur most often in the central part of the United States.   E. R. B.

SEE ALSO: CLOUD, WEATHER

Torque (TAWRK) When a body is acted upon by a force that tends to produce rotation of the body, the result is called the *moment of force,* or *torque.* The value of torque is equal to the force itself multiplied by the perpendicular distance from the line of action of the force to the axis of rotation. This distance is often called the *lever arm* of the force, and the line around which the body rotates is known as the *axis of rotation.*

As an example, consider opening or closing a door. The axis of rotation is the line passing through the hinges. Now, if one pushes against the knob, the force causes the door to rotate on its hinges. Thus, the force must have created a torque. If one pushes on the door at a point closer to the hinges than the knob, a greater force is required than before because the length of the lever arm has been decreased. The distance from force to hinge is less than from knob to hinge.

Now suppose that a bar is pivoted at its center. If a force is exerted on one end of the bar and an equal but opposite force is exerted on the other end, the result will be a turning of the bar. This combination of forces is called a *couple.* A couple is properly defined as a pair of equal forces acting in opposite but parallel lines. The torque produced by the couple will be F times l, where "l" is the perpendicular distance between the forces. Its value will be the same regardless of where the fulcrum is placed.

To simplify the mathematical treatment of torques, a rule known as the *torque rule* is used. It is stated as follows: the sum of

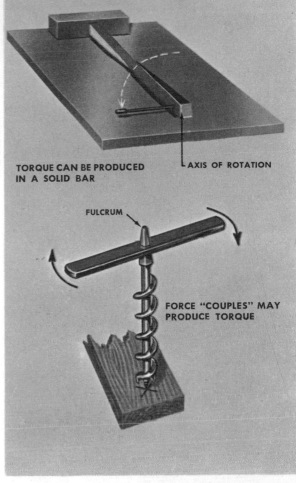

TORQUE CAN BE PRODUCED IN A SOLID BAR — AXIS OF ROTATION

FULCRUM

FORCE "COUPLES" MAY PRODUCE TORQUE

the torques acting on any point of a body must be zero (cancel each other out) if the body is to remain in rotational equilibrium. The torque tending to turn a body in a counter-clockwise direction is called a *positive* torque, and the clockwise rotation is called a *negative* torque. It is also true that the sum of the positive torques must be equal to the sum of the negative torques if the body is not to rotate.   A. E. L.

SEE ALSO: FOOT-POUND; MACHINES, SIMPLE; TORSION; WORK

Torricelli, Evangelista see Barometer

Torsion (TAWR-shun) The STRESS required to twist a solid body, such as a metal rod or a wire, is called torsion. Rotating shafts in machines (or parts of structures which undergo stress of this sort) must be tested so that the shaft will not be placed under too much TORQUE (force which tends to twist the shaft).

Tortoise see Turtle

Helen J. Challand
Touch-me-not is valued for its bright flowers

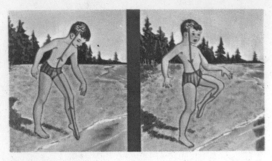

Reaction to cold water involves both the tactile organs and heat receptors

Touch Touch is the sense which enables animals to feel pressure or motion of a solid, liquid, or gas (air movements). The sense of touch can also recognize variation of temperature or differences in such characteristics or objects as shape, texture, or size. All people have this sense, but in some it is better developed than in others.

Stimuli are received by special organs, known as *tactile corpuscles,* which are found in the skin. These organs are sensitive to changes in pressure. They send impulses along nerves to the central NERVOUS SYSTEM which, in turn, causes a muscular reaction or other response, by sending impulses to muscles controlling the part.

Tactile corpuscles are found in greater numbers in the finger tips and the tip of the tongue than elsewhere in the body. The upper back is so thinly provided with tactile corpuscles that certain areas can be touched with a fine point and not be felt. The sensitivity of an area depends upon the number of corpuscles present. Blind persons, or those using the sense of touch in occupations, develop this sense more than the average person. Blocking of impulses by anesthesia, or cutting nerves, eliminates this sense.   D. J. I.

Touch-me-not Touch-me-nots are plants known by many names. Sometimes they are called *jewelweeds, snapweeds,* or *impatiens.* They are succulent plants that belong to the *garden balsam* family. Touch-me-nots are easy to grow.

Touch-me-nots are native to Asia, tropical Africa, and tropical North America. *Impatiens,* one name for this plant, is a Latin word meaning "impatient." The seed pods of these plants seem to be impatient to scatter their seeds, and burst open quite easily.   M. R. L.

Tourmaline Tourmaline is a very complex silicate and occurs in several crystalline forms. The crystals are found in a variety of colors; black and brown are the most common. The tourmaline used for GEMS may be green, blue, deep red, pink, or black.

Tourmaline is a compound of silica, boron, aluminum, and water; it often also contains iron, magnesium, sodium, or lithium, and occasionally fluorine. Tourmaline has a hardness of 7 to 7.5 on the Mohs HARDNESS SCALE. The crystals are generally brittle, although gem tourmaline is less so than the other types. Crystals are used in pressure gauges because they exhibit the PIEZOELECTRIC EFFECT.   D. A. B.
SEE ALSO: MINERALS

Tourniquet see First aid

Toxin see Poison, Vaccine

Tracer see Nuclear science glossary

Trachea see Respiratory system

Tourmaline crystal with the two minerals albite and lepidolite, from California

J. Daniel Williams

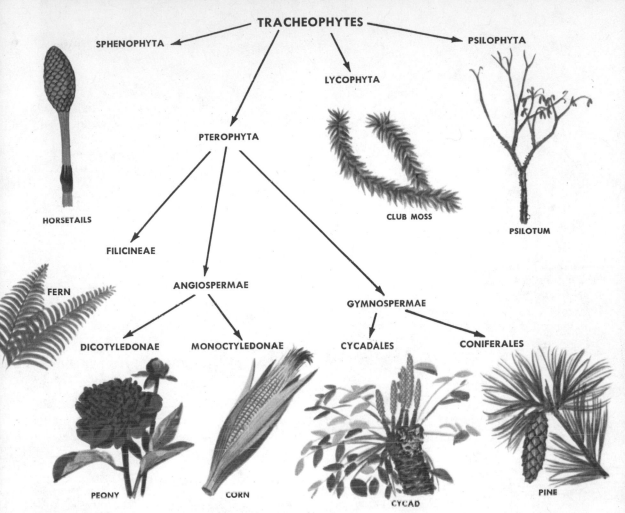

TRACHEOPHYTES

SPHENOPHYTA

PSILOPHYTA

LYCOPHYTA

PTEROPHYTA

HORSETAILS

CLUB MOSS

PSILOTUM

FILICINEAE

ANGIOSPERMAE

GYMNOSPERMAE

FERN

DICOTYLEDONAE

MONOCTYLEDONAE

CYCADALES

CONIFERALES

PEONY

CORN

CYCAD

PINE

Tracheophytes (TRAY-kee-oh-fytes) The Plant Kingdom is divided into several large groups. The tracheophytes (Phylum *Tracheophyta*) are a group of plants that have a network of pipe-like cells that connect the leaves, stems, and roots.

The pipes that bring water and minerals up from the roots through the stem into the leaves are made of *xylem* cells. The living parts of these cells die as the plant grows, and there are left hollow spaces within the thick cell walls.

The *phloem* is the name given to the pipes that carry the food, which is made in the leaves, downward through the stem and into the root for nourishment and storage. These PHLOEM cells are alive, but also have hollow spaces. The cells are connected by sievelike plates. The phloem lies outside the XYLEM.

This network of pipe-lines, called a *vascular system,* has made it possible for plants to live on land. Since plants depend so com-pletely on water to stay alive, there must be a way to bring water to all parts of the plant. As long as a plant lives completely surrounded by water or in moist, humid places, the water supply is not a problem. When plants move into the dry air, however, a vascular system becomes necessary.

The first tracheophytes were very simple land-living plants. These plants are no longer living on Earth, but they grew 280 million years ago at the time when the first amphibians came into existence.

The tracheophyte plants that are living today include the club mosses, the horsetails, the ferns, and the seed plants. The seed plants are the best developed of all plants, and owe part of their great success to their excellent vascular systems. Spruce, pine, and redwood trees, as well as oak, maple, and birch trees are among those that have risen to towering heights in the forests of the world. The flowering plants of woods, meadows, and gardens, numbering thousands of species, provide a beautiful display of this great phylum. B. B. G.

SEE ALSO: PLANTS, CLASSIFICATION OF

Trade winds Trade winds are steady, strong winds that blow across the Atlantic and Pacific oceans. In the Northern Hemisphere, they blow from the northeast toward the southwest; in the Southern Hemisphere, from the southeast toward the northwest. These winds have a definite path, from about 30° N. latitude to about 30° S. latitude, shifting slightly with the seasons.

As far back as 1686, EDMUND HALLEY of England correctly explained the trade winds. He said that they were caused by the constant heat in the equatorial regions: air always flows from a cool area to a hot area, and since the equator is the hottest zone on earth, the ocean winds flow toward it. They are turned westward by the rotation of the earth, but only blow across the oceans because they are stopped by the land.

The molecular theory of heat affords further explanation of the trade winds. The air molecules in the hot air near the equator are moving and smashing into each other harder and faster than the air molecules at higher latitudes. The equatorial air, therefore, balloons upward (causing the calms near the equator) and leaves an area of low pressure (fewer air molecules). Air from the north and south then rushes in to take its place. As the warm, rising air sprays out toward the north and the south, there is less contact between molecules, causing loss of heat. Some of the cooling air descends at about latitudes 30° north and south of the equator (the HORSE LATITUDES), spreading out into a northbound and southbound flow of air. The winds that flow toward the equator, twisted by the earth's rotation, are the famous trade winds, the steadiest winds known.   H. W. M.

SEE ALSO: HEAT, MOLECULAR THEORY, WEATHER, WIND

Trailing arbutus (ahr-BYOO-tuhs) Trailing arbutus, or *mayflower,* is an evergreen plant that is related to azaleas, rhododendrons, and laurels. This slightly woody perennial spreads along the ground. It has very fragrant pink or white flowers that grow in thick clusters.

The thick leaves are pointed or blunt at the tip, and heart-shaped or rounded near the stem. The fleshy, almost round, fruit splits open at maturity.

Trailing arbutus grows in rocky or sandy soil in the woods of Canada, and as far south as Florida.   D. C. H.

Train, railroad The railroad train consists of a locomotive which moves attached passenger or freight cars over fixed rails. The basic purpose of this vehicle is to transport people and materials in large volume at little cost.

Railroad trains were first constructed in the United States about 1826, but at first they were horse-drawn. Simple steam locomotives had been used in England as early as 1803 to haul coal from the mines. Industry was growing very fast, and people saw the possibilities of the train for hauling raw materials and products, carrying mail, and speeding up travel. In the early 1830's, the steam locomotive was perfected as a self-powered mover. Within one hundred years the railroad train became a fast, quiet, smokeless and comfortable means of transportation, and a major freight carrier.

Great flexibility of rail car movement has been accomplished by the adoption of a standard gauge, or width, of 4 feet 8½ inches between rails. When railroads were first built, as many as twenty-three different gauges were used. Now, trains can travel from Canada to Mexico without hindrance by odd-gauged tracks.

RAILROAD LOCOMOTIVES

The locomotive is a power plant on wheels designed to pull or push a number of railroad cars. It may generate its own POWER by producing steam by burning fuel, or it may be powered from overhead or by third-rail electrical systems.

The steam-engine propelled locomotives, which were the first type used, have been

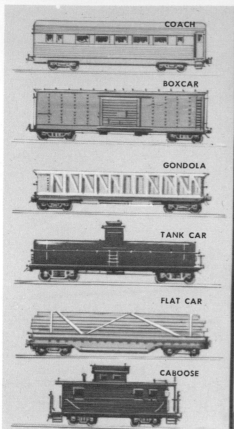

COACH

BOXCAR

GONDOLA

TANK CAR

FLAT CAR

CABOOSE

replaced by the diesel locomotives only within the past twenty-five years. Of the 33,000 locomotives now operating in the United States, only twelve per cent are run by steam, whereas eighty-five per cent are run by diesel power plants. Diesel engines are more efficient than other types, and they use low-cost heavy oil. The remaining three per cent consists of electric and gasoline TURBINE locomotives.

The characteristics required for the locomotive depend upon its use. For example, passenger locomotives are designed for pulling relatively light loads, with fast acceleration and at high speeds. Since the pulling capacity of the locomotive depends to a great extent upon its weight and resulting friction of the wheels with the rails, this type of locomotive need not be as heavy as freight locomotives.

Freight locomotives pull very heavy loads, with slower acceleration and speeds than passenger locomotives. In order to increase the power required to pull a train, several locomotives are often coupled together to function as one unit.

Beside the amount of traction developed at the driving wheels, several other characteristics limit the pulling capacity of the locomotive. A locomotive pulling 100 freight cars totalling 7000 tons would re-

quire a pulling capacity of 21,000 pounds on level track once the train had reached a steady speed. For every one-foot rise in 100 feet of track (1% grade), the locomotive must pull an additional 20 pounds per ton —in this instance, an extra load of 140,000 pounds. Similarly, curves offer a resistance of about ½ pound per ton for each degree of curvature. In order to accelerate the train one mile per hour each second, it would be necessary to add a pull of 100 pounds per ton of train.

For these reasons, grades (slopes) are usually kept below 2%. Tracks are laid as straight as possible. Trains have so much INERTIA that they speed up very slowly.

RAILROAD CARS

Railroad cars serve to convey either passengers or freight. Passenger cars include (1) coaches, which accommodate 50 to 80 people on fixed or reclining seats; (2) sleeping cars, which provide varying types of bedroom arrangements; (3) dining cars, which supply restaurants on wheels; and (4) lounge and observation cars, which afford entertainment and places for relaxation. Normally, mail and baggage cars are also part of the passenger train.

There are several kinds of freight cars. *Boxcars* look like a box with large sliding doors at the center of each side. Most materials, especially those requiring protection from weather, are shipped in this type of car. A variation is the well-insulated *refrigerator car* used for transporting perishable items such as meat, fish, and flowers. *Flatcars* have flat floors and no sides or top. They carry items which will not fit in a boxcar. *Gondola cars* have four sides but no top. Bulk materials such as coal, sand, and scrap metal are transported in these cars. *Hopper cars* are similar to gondola cars, but they have trap doors in the floor to speed the emptying of bulk materials. *Tank cars* are cylindrical tanks used to haul many types of liquids. Perhaps the most familiar car is the *caboose,* attached to the end of the freight train. It houses the train crew and provides a vantage point to view operation of the train.   E. I. D.

SEE ALSO: ENGINES, MOMENTUM

Trajectory see Astronautics

Tranquilizer A tranquilizer is a DRUG which calms excitement and tension. It does not affect the respiratory muscles, or cause addiction, but it does produce some undesirable side effects. Chlorpromazine and reserpine were the' first tranquilizers used in treatment of mental distress.

Transformer A transformer is a device for increasing or decreasing the voltage in an AC electrical circuit. For example, a transformer is used to lower the voltage supplied at the wall outlet to a voltage suitable for operating model trains or other electrical toys.

A transformer consists of two separate, insulated coils of copper wire, wound upon a magnetic steel frame, or *core.* The first coil, or *primary winding,* is connected to the source of current to be altered in voltage. The current within the primary coil alternately magnetizes the core in opposite directions. This constantly changing *magnetic field,* when passing through a secondary coil, or winding, induces a voltage in the secondary by the law of electromagnetic induction. A transformer cannot be used in a DC system, since electro-magnetic induction depends upon a constantly changing current.

The voltage induced in the secondary winding is equal to the voltage of the primary times the ratio of the number of turns on the secondary to the number of turns on the primary winding. When the secondary has more turns than the primary, the voltage induced in the secondary is greater than that of the source, and the transformer is a *step-up* transformer. When there are fewer turns on the secondary, a lower voltage is induced and the transformer is a *step-down* transformer. A step-up transformer steps up the voltage, but not the total energy because watts equal volts times amperes; and amperes are reduced when volts are increased.

Transformers are important in the communications and power industries.   C. F. R.

SEE ALSO: ELECTRICITY, ELECTROMAGNET

IRON CORE

ALTERNATING CURRENT INPUT

ALTERNATING CURRENT OUTPUT

STEP DOWN TRANSFORMER

AC

STEP DOWN TRANSFORMER (2 TO 1)

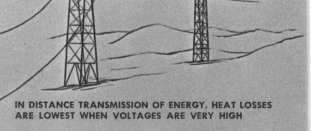

AC

STEP UP TRANSFORMER (1 TO 2)

IN DISTANCE TRANSMISSION OF ENERGY, HEAT LOSSES ARE LOWEST WHEN VOLTAGES ARE VERY HIGH

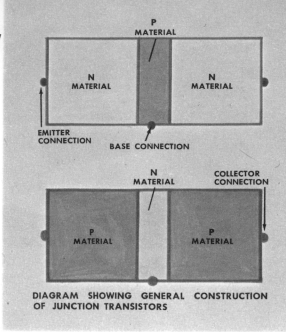

DIAGRAM SHOWING GENERAL CONSTRUCTION OF JUNCTION TRANSISTORS

Transfusion (trans-FEW-zhun) Transfusion means to put, or transfer, blood from one living body into the body of another. The person giving the blood is called a *donor*. When transfusions are given to humans, the blood of the donor must match the BLOOD of the patient or death may occur.

There are four kinds of human blood. Except for one type (O), which can be mixed with any type of blood, they cannot be mixed. Mixing the three other types of blood causes red blood cells to clump. If too much clumping occurs after a transfusion, the patient may die. In hospitals a patient's blood is typed, or matched, to blood from a donor before a transfusion.

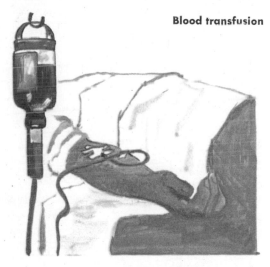

Blood transfusion

At one time, blood transfusions were made directly from the blood vessel of a donor into the vein of a patient. Today it is possible to store blood in hospital blood banks. A patient using some of this blood must replace the amount used with blood from a healthy person.

At the present time the meaning of the word "transfusion" is not restricted to blood. It covers all kinds of solutions, such as sugars or plasmas, transfused into a CIRCULATORY SYSTEM.

Different types of blood occur among other vertebrates, such as cats, dogs, monkeys, and chickens. The differences are probably not as great as among humans since veterinarians do not have to type blood before giving transfusions. J. C. K.
SEE ALSO: BLOOD TYPES

Transistor (tran-ZISST-er) The transistor is one of the devices which make it possible for a small amount of electrical energy to control a much greater amount. Transistors are made of specially prepared silicon, germanium, or other *semiconductors*. (A semiconductor is a substance which offers less resistance to electric current flow than an insulator but more resistance than a conductor.) When the proper voltages are applied to a transistor, electric charges *already present* within the semiconductor are moved, creating a current flow.

The *junction* transistor is the most important form in present use. It is made as a "sandwich" of two different alloys of germanium, n-germanium and p-germanium. The thin "filler" of the sandwich, the base of the transistor, is made of one material and is sandwiched between slices of the other material. Junction transistors may be either n-p-n or p-n-p transistors; each type offers advantages in certain applications. The electric current in n-germanium is electron flow. In p-germanium, however, the electric current consists of the travel of positively-charged regions, called *holes,* which exist only in semiconductors. The entire transistor is a single crystal of germanium with the proper *impurities* added to make the "sandwich."

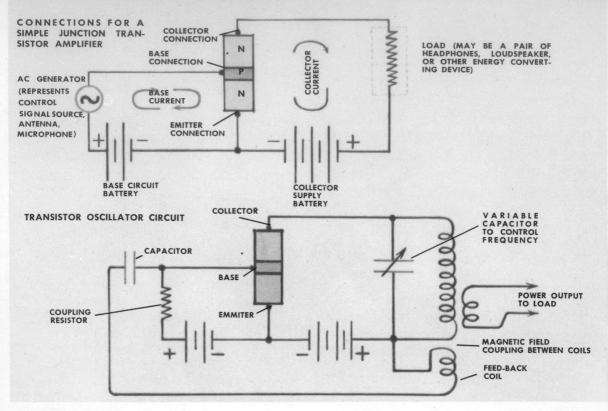

CONNECTIONS FOR A SIMPLE JUNCTION TRANSISTOR AMPLIFIER

COLLECTOR CONNECTION

BASE CONNECTION

N
P
N

COLLECTOR CURRENT

LOAD (MAY BE A PAIR OF HEADPHONES, LOUDSPEAKER, OR OTHER ENERGY CONVERTING DEVICE)

AC GENERATOR (REPRESENTS CONTROL SIGNAL SOURCE, ANTENNA, MICROPHONE)

BASE CURRENT

EMITTER CONNECTION

BASE CIRCUIT BATTERY

COLLECTOR SUPPLY BATTERY

TRANSISTOR OSCILLATOR CIRCUIT

COLLECTOR

CAPACITOR

BASE

COUPLING RESISTOR

EMMITER

VARIABLE CAPACITOR TO CONTROL FREQUENCY

POWER OUTPUT TO LOAD

MAGNETIC FIELD COUPLING BETWEEN COILS

FEED-BACK COIL

To simplify the description, an n-p-n transistor will be described. The p-n-p transistor connected in a circuit operates similarly. The battery connections are reversed when a p-n-p transistor is used. When the base circuit battery is correctly adjusted, only a limited amount of current can flow from emitter to the collector terminals through the transistor and thus through the load. When the AC generator (representing a signal source) makes the base region more positive, more current flows from the emitter to the collector, and then through the load. When the base is made more negative, the collector and load current decreases.

Since the changes in the emitter-collector current may be from ten to one hundred times greater than the changes in the base current which caused them, the transistor is a powerful *signal amplifier,* or *step-up* device. Thus one transistor can amplify the power of an AC signal as much as one hundred times. When even greater amplification is needed, several transistors can be operated in a cascade pattern (one after another).

The circuit just described is called the *common-base* circuit since the base is common to both input and output circuits. A transistor can also be connected with the collector common to both input and output circuits (common collector circuit) or with the emitter common to both circuits (common emitter circuit). The choice of one circuit arrangement over another is usually dictated by what is desired.

If a transistor amplifier is connected so that some of the amplified signal is fed back into the input circuit in the proper phase, the amplifier will become an oscillator. An oscillator is a circuit that converts DC into AC, usually at a frequency much greater than could possibly be developed by an ordinary electromechanical generator. Oscillators are used to generate electrical signals in RADIO, TELEVISION, and RADAR circuits.

Transistors are also used as high-speed switching devices in computers and in telephone central offices. The switching ability of a transistor is one of its most important characteristics.

Transistors are still used somewhat less frequently than electron tubes. Transistors are smaller than tubes and require far lower operating voltages, but they are more expensive, delicate, and highly sensitive to excess heat and radiation. Semiconductor materials other than germanium and silicon are being tried in an effort to overcome some of the disadvantages. Compounds such as gallium arsenide, indium antimonide, and silicon carbide show promise as transistor materials.   C. F. R.

SEE ALSO: ELECTRICITY, ELECTRONICS, PHOTOELECTRICITY

Translucent Translucent describes a material which diffuses or spreads rays of LIGHT which pass through it. Light can pass through it but objects cannot be seen clearly through it. It is only partly transparent.

Transmission see Automobile

Transmutation of elements This process changes one element into another. It occurs in natural radioactivity. Scientists can accomplish transmutation by bombarding an element with high-speed particles generated by NUCLEAR REACTORS.
SEE: ALCHEMY, NUCLEAR ENERGY, NUCLEAR SCIENCE

Transonic see Supersonic

Transparent Transparent is a term commonly used to describe a material which lets the visible rays of the spectrum through it in such a way that the material can be seen through. Other materials are transparent to other kinds of radiation, such as ultra-violet rays.
SEE: LIGHT

Transpiration (trans-pih-RAY-shun) Man gives off water through his skin. This process is called *perspiration*. Plants give off water through their leaves in a similar process called *transpiration*. On a hot summer day a man can lose two pints of water by perspiration. A single corn plant transpires two quarts a day. A giant redwood tree loses gallons of water a day through transpiration.

The minerals in the soil must be dissolved in water before they can enter the root cells. A plant must take in much more water than it needs to get enough minerals to make food. Since the plant cannot hold all this water, it lets the water out through little holes in the leaves.

The roots are continually absorbing water through their root hairs. This water

* **THINGS TO DO**

DO PLANTS GIVE OFF WATER?

1 Tie a clear plastic bag over the leaves and stem of a plant. Be sure none of the plant touches the bag except where it is tied securely around the stem just above the soil level.
2 Set it in the sun for several hours.
3 Observe what happens in the bag. Where does the water come from?

forms columns in the tubes and vessels from the roots to the leaves. Many of the cells in the leaf are next to air spaces. These spaces open to the outside through minute holes called stomata pores. Each is surrounded by two cells (*guard* cells) which control the opening and closing of the pore. As water leaves the cells, it exerts a pull on the water behind it. This transpirational pull is exerted from one cell to another and helps this long column of water to be pulled upward from the roots to the leaves. A plant uses only about ten per cent of the water absorbed. The excess water is transpired. An acre of corn will lose 8000 gallons in a single day. A corn plant needs 500 pounds of water to make one pound of plant. Alfalfa needs 900 pounds of water, while the cactus needs only 40 pounds of water to make one pound of cactus.

There are several factors which affect the rate of transpiration. The following conditions increase transpiration: larger leaves, thin cuticle on leaves, greater number of stomata per square inch, low humidity in the surrounding air, strong wind currents, higher temperature, bright sunny weather, and lower air pressure. If the roots do not absorb at the same rate as transpiration occurs, the balance is upset. This causes dehydration or wilting because of the loss of *turgor* in the plant cells. H. J. C.
SEE ALSO: PLANT, STOMATA

TRANSPLANTING SEEDLINGS

1 Before moving seedlings outside, prepare the garden soil for the new plants by cultivating and working in leaf mold or compost fertilizer.
2 Dissolve one cup of any plant food that dissolves quickly into twelve quarts of water.
3 Dig a hole larger than the width of the roots. Pour a little solution in it.
4 With a tool, lift up the young seedling, being careful not to shake the soil off the roots. The fine root-hairs may be destroyed if soil is removed. Set the plant in the hole.
5 Fill the hole with loose, dry soil. Water again, but do not pack the soil down after this last watering.

CARING FOR ROOT-BOUND PLANTS

As a potted plant grows, the root system becomes larger. Soon the plant becomes root-bound. This may be detected when the feeding roots reach out to the sides of the pot or begin to grow out of the drainage hole in the bottom of the pot.

1 Secure a larger container. Place an inch of coarse gravel or broken pieces of clay flower pots in the bottom. Add an inch of soil.
2 Turn over the potted plant and tap the container it is in on the edge of a table. The ball of soil and roots will drop out.
3 Place the plant in the larger pot, fill with good soil, and water well.

Transplanting Just as a child gets too big for his clothes, so does a plant outgrow the size of the pot in which it is living. A plant may need to be moved or transplanted to a larger pot to let its roots spread out. Plants planted inside need to be moved outside and planted in the garden when the weather is warmer. Transplanting, then, means to move a plant from one area to another or from one container to another.

Transplanting may destroy part of the root system and upset the balance between ABSORPTION and TRANSPIRATION. The plant continues to lose water through the leaves and there is less root surface to absorb the moisture needed. To remedy this, keep the newly transplanted specimen in a shaded area, reduce the temperature, and water it frequently. H. J. C.

Transuranium elements The transuranium elements, all in the actinide series, range from NEPTUNIUM, element 93, to element 103. They resemble the rare earths. They are produced by bombarding the atoms of other elements, and are radioactive.
SEE: ELEMENTS

Encysted trichina worm in muscle tissue

Tree of heaven The tree of heaven is the common name for the *ailanthus* tree. It has long, compound leaves with many long, thin, pointed leaflets. It looks like an overgrown fern. It can grow rapidly and strongly even from a little bit of poor soil near a sidewalk in a city.

The ailanthus blooms in June. Its flowers are thin sprays of small, yellowish blossoms. Some trees produce male, pollen-bearing blossoms and others produce the female, seed-bearing flowers. If the leaves or the staminate flowers are crushed, they give off a strong, disagreeable odor. The pollen flowers fall off, but the seed flowers mature into large, brilliant bunches of seeds. Where a leaf falls from the tree, the branch is left with a gray scar that is shaped like a shield.　　C. L. K.

Tree of heaven can grow in little soil

Trench mouth Trench mouth, or *Vincent's angina,* is a disease of the mouth in which the gums, the lining of the cheeks, and the floor of the mouth become dark red, swollen, and sore. It is called "trench mouth" because during World War I soldiers in the trenches had the disease.

Triangle sec Geometry

Triassic see Mesozoic Era, Geologic time table

Trichina (trih-KYE-nuh) Trichinae are slender roundworms which may be found in hogs, bears, rats, and humans. The larvae of these small worms are parasites, which means they cannot live freely in nature. The worms pass from one animal to another in pork or bear meat which has not been well-cooked. The young, which are produced in the intestine, make their way to various muscles where they coil up and harden. Only prolonged heat will kill the worms in muscle tissue.

Adult worms are encysted in the muscles of pork and enter a person's disgestive tract when undercooked pork is eaten. The worms lay hundreds of eggs in the intestines. As the larvae develop they begin to migrate throughout the body. They bore through the wall of the human intestine and enter the blood and lymph vessels. They leave these structures looking like perforated sieves in their journey to the muscles. The larvae usually end up in the muscles of the rib, tongue, eye, and diaphragm. They remain there, grow into adults, and die unless this muscle is eaten by another animal.

An animal with trichina worms is said to have *trichinosis.* Since the worms are microscopic, it is impossible for the United States Governmental agencies to inspect the meat for contamination. The only safeguard against the *Trichinella* worm is thorough cooking of pork.　　H. J. C.

SEE ALSO: NEMATHELMINTHES, PARASITES

Trichinosis see Trichina

Trichocyst A trichocyst is a tiny capsule containing a hair-like stinging organ. It is found in some protozoans, such as the PARAMECIUM.

Trigonometry see Mathematics

Trillium see Wild flowers

Trilobites, ancient three-lobed animals

Trilobite (TRY-luh-byte) Trilobites were a large group of animals that lived in the ocean. They are now extinct. For thousands of years there were probably more trilobites than any other animal in the ocean. Then the other animals that were better adapted came along. The little trilobites began to disappear.

The name "trilobite" means "having three lobes." The many segments of the animal's body were covered from head to tail by three sections of shell. The shell was made of CHITIN—a hard, nonliving substance. Trilobites were able to roll up in their shells for protection. Most trilobites were only an inch or two long. Some, though, got to be over a foot long. They all lived either on the ocean floor or burrowed into the sand.

Trilobites were among the first members of Phylum *Arthropoda*—the group including crayfish, lobsters and insects. During the Paleozoic Era, there were about 1000 genera and 2000 species of trilobites. One of the main differences among them was in the size and placement of a *suture,* or slit, in the head end of the chitin. When the animal started molting so that it could grow, the first crack in the chitin was from this suture. After shedding the shell, the animal grew and then secreted a new shell.

Many fossils of many kinds of trilobites have been found. Because they are so numerous and from such a definite period in the past, they are often used as *index fossils* for dating Cambrian and other Paleozoic rocks.   J. F. B.

SEE ALSO: EVOLUTION, GEOLOGIC TIME TABLE, PALEONTOLOGY

Triplets see Multiple births

Tritium see Hydrogen

Tropical climate see Climate

Tropical fish The tropics are the very warm lands and waters near the equator. Many kinds of fish live in the warm water. These fish, which are called tropical fish, are beautiful in shape and color. They are so pretty that many people like to collect them and keep them at home in aquariums.

Tropical fish are either marine fish, which means they live in the ocean in salty water, or fresh-water fish, which usually means they live in rivers, streams, and ponds. A marine fish cannot live in fresh water, and a fresh-water fish cannot live in salty, ocean water.

Like most plants and animals that live in the tropics, tropical fish are found in almost endless variety. Colorful reds, silvers, blues, greens, purples—even blacks and glowing fluorescents which sparkle at night —almost every color imaginable can be found in the tropical-fish world. There are the stately, slow-moving angel fish, the speed-demon striped zebras, the friendly kissing gouramis, the ferocious piranhas, the aggressive barbs—gentle, family-loving fish-parents and destructive bullies. The habits of fish are as different and as interesting as the habits of people.

Tropical fish are divided into four groups by their mating habits: the egg-layers, the live-bearers, the bubble-nest builders, and the cichlids.

Egg-layers drop eggs, which later hatch into young fish, in the water. This group includes many beautiful and unusual fish. The butterfly fish has large pectoral fins which allow it to soar out of the water as a "flying fish." The hatchet fish has a bulging belly which is paper-thin when viewed from the front. The blind cave fish and the fierce piranha belong to this group. The

Zebras are egg-laying tropical fish

SOME COMMON TROPICAL FISH

1—ANGEL FISH
2—NEON TETRAS
3—TROPICAL CATFISH
4—SIAMESE FIGHTING FISH
5—PLATY, OR MOON FISH
6—FISH HAVE NO EARS. THEY HEAR WITH THEIR BODIES TAKING VIBRATION FROM THE WATER
7—FEMALE SWORDTAIL
8—BLOODFINS

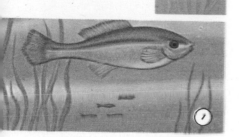

bloodfins; the sparkling, colorful tetras; the glowing rasboras; and the playful barbs are among the most popular of tropical fish. The eel-like knife fish and loaches are interesting additions to the aquarium, as are the bottom-feeding, whiskered catfish, and especially the leopard-spotted corydoras.

The *live-bearers* hatch their eggs inside the body of the female. The young are released as free-swimming babies. This group includes many aquarium favorites: the tiny irridescent guppies; the beautiful mollies which have large, sail-like dorsal fins; the attractive platys of varied colors; and the arresting swordtail with its brilliant color and long, streaming anal fin. In this group of fish, the males are the spectacular specimens, while the females are less showy.

It is fascinating to watch the *bubble-nest builders*. These fish have air-breathing organs, and normally take bubbles of air into their mouths. At breeding time, the male makes a cradle of sudsy air bubbles on the surface of the water. After mating, the male picks up each egg in its mouth, forms an air bubble around it, and delivers it to the floating nest. It is also the father who tends the nest and guards the young after they hatch. The mother is driven into a corner in submission. The magnificent paradise fish, Siamese fighting fish (betta), and gouramis are members of this group.

The *cichlids* have a highly organized mating behavior. During courtship, the male and female interlock by the jaws into a struggling embrace. If they both outlast this athletic contest, they mate. The eggs are laid in a carefully prepared nesting spot. Then both parents participate in transferring the eggs, a few at a time, from one depression to another that has been prepared in the sand. Some of these fish are mouthbreeders and keep the entire brood in their mouths for as long as 15 days until they have all hatched. It is believed that this mouth care is a kind of "baby bath" which frees the eggs of fungus, a dangerous scourge. The angel fish, the jewel fish, the pompadour fish, and the Egyptian mouthbreeder are some of the better-known cichlids.

B. B. G.

SEE ALSO: AQUARIUM, GOLDFISH, GUPPY

Tropical plants see Plants, tropical

Tropics see Cancer (constellation), Capricornus, Earth

IN WHICH DIRECTION DO ROOTS GROW?

1   Put a layer of cotton on a piece of glass. Place several seeds in a row across the center of the cotton. Corn, bean, and radish seeds will germinate quickly.

2   Put a second piece of glass over the seeds and cotton, thus making a sandwich.

3   Tie the glass together, and set it on end in a dish of water.

4   In two or three days the small seedlings will appear. In which direction are the roots growing?

5   After the first week turn the glass sandwich around so the top edge is immersed in the water. Notice the roots are pointing up and the little shoot downward. After a week in this position which part of the plant is growing down toward the center of the earth?

Tropism (TRO-pizm) Tropism is the turning of a plant toward or away from something. Plants lean toward the light. Roots grow toward water. Most stems grow away from the earth. On a sunny, summer day some plants will fold up their leaves. These movements by plants help them get the materials they need to live. They are not able to run around like most animals to get food or get away from things that endanger their lives.

The word tropism comes from the Greek word *tropos,* which means to turn. Parts of different plants may react differently to the same outside stimulus. For example, roots grow toward the earth's center which is positive *geotropism.* A prefix in front of the word *tropic* indicates the outside stimulus to which the plant will react. *Phototropic* means the response to light, *hydrotropic* to water, *chemotropic* to chemicals, *thermotropic* to changes in temperature, *thigmotropic* to touch, and *electrotropic* to current. This irritability toward things in its environment enables a plant to secure the needed raw materials and energy for survival. It is also a safety mechanism to avoid injury. Some leaves will curl up in bright sunlight to slow down the rate of water loss in TRANSPIRATION. Roots will grow away from copper sewer pipes. *Traumatotropism* is the ability to grow scar tissue over a wound to prevent any foreign material from entering.

Tropisms can be explained by understanding the action of a plant hormone *auxin* on plant cells. This hormone controls the growth and other physiological activities. Auxin increases the rate of cell growth. A house plant set in a window receives more light on one side, but the other side is shaded. Since light inhibits the action of auxin, the cells on the side of the plant away from the direct sun grow faster. This causes the plant to lean toward the source of light.   H. J. C.

SEE ALSO: PLANT

Troposphere see Atmosphere

Phototropism, the response to light, can be seen by turning a plant in a window

Trout A trout is a food and game fish. It is usually found in cold, fresh water in lakes and streams, but a few species live in the ocean. There are more than thirty species in American waters. They eat insects, worms, minnows and other small fish.

The *lake trout* is the largest of the trout family. It is commercially important in the Great Lakes region. Trout may weigh as much as eighty pounds, but usually weigh between five and ten pounds.

Chicago Natural History Museum

Lake trout (top) and brook trout

The brook trout is the most beautiful and widely distributed of the trout family. It usually weighs less than three pounds, although some weigh more.

Trout have long, fine-scaled bodies, scaleless heads, and two soft-rayed dorsal, or back fins. The fighting trout is a favorite game fish, especially in the United States where government hatcheries keep streams abundantly supplied. One of the handsomest and gamiest of trout is the *rainbow* trout, usually found in the rushing streams of the western states. M. R. L.

Tsetse fly see Fly, Sleeping sickness

Rainbow trout

Chicago Natural History Museum

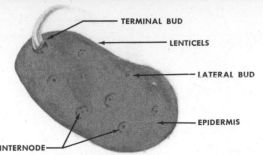

TERMINAL BUD
LENTICELS
LATERAL BUD
EPIDERMIS
INTERNODE

The potato, a tuber, illustrates how all stems, whether above or below ground, are similar to each other in structure

Tuber Tuber is a swollen part at the end of an underground STEM of a plant. The tuber holds the food for the plant. The POTATO is a tuber.

All of the plant but the tuber usually dies when winter comes. The tuber lies dormant until spring when it sprouts at the *nodes,* where the buds or eyes develop. *Internodes* are the spaces between the eyes. The young shoots reach above the ground to form new plants and obtain food from the tuber until their own roots and leaves are formed.

The eyes of the potato appear in a spiral pattern that circles the tuber. Tubers of other plants do not necessarily sprout in a definite pattern. Each eye consists of a ridge holding a tiny, scale-like leaf and usually three buds. Potatoes are usually propagated by planting a piece of potato with one or more eyes.

The tuber is scarred where it breaks from the *apex,* or tip, of the underground stem. This is sometimes called the *rhizome* of the plant. P. G. B.

Tuberculosis (two-BUR-kew-LOW-sis) Tuberculosis, or "TB", is a disease that can be passed from one person to another. It is caused by a bacterium (*Mycobacterium tuberculosis*), which makes odd cell growths called *tubercles* form in body tissues. The germ is usually spread by the sputum of the infected person.

Any portion of the body, the bones, the skin, or the spinal column, may be affected, but the disease usually attacks the lungs and is then called *pulmonary* tuberculosis. Symptoms are fatigue, loss of weight, low fever that appears in the evening, and a chronic cough. Today, X-ray examinations can reveal the presence of the disease and the *tuberculin* test shows if a person was ever exposed to the disease. J. M. C.

Tuberose is a summer-flowering garden plant

Tuberose (TOOB-rohs) The French use Mexican tuberose to make perfume. It is grown in the United States as a garden plant. The fragrant flowers are waxy and white, and appear in the fall. The plant grows to a height of two to three feet.

Tuberoses depend upon an underground stem, a *tuber,* to propagate itself. This structure stores up food for the next year. Usually the productive life is about five years. It is necessary to dig up the tubers before the first killing frost and store them until spring. D. C. H.

Tuberous begonia see Begonia

Tufted titmouse see Titmouse

Tularemia see Animal diseases

Courtesy Society For Visual Education, Inc.
Single (top) and double-petaled tulips

Tulips have attractive blue-green foliage
F. A. Blashfield

Tulip The brightly colored tulip is one of the first flowers to bloom in the spring. The flower and long leaves grow from a bulb or underground stem. Each spring for several years the bulb produces one beautiful flower. Tulips bloom in almost every color from white to a blue so dark that it looks black. Some are streaked with other colors.

While there are over sixty species and countless varieties of cultivated tulips, there are no known wild species of this garden plant.

Since tulips belong to the *lily* family, they have six stamens and one compound pistil originating from several leaf-like parts (*carpels*). Tulip leaves seem to grow directly from the ground since very little of the plant stem is above the ground.

The word *tulip* comes from the Persian word for *turban*. The plant was grown extensively in Turkey, coming to Vienna, Austria, from Constantinople in the 1500's. Today most of the bulbs are produced in the Netherlands. J. C. K.

Field of single tulips

Courtesy Society For Visual Education, Inc.

Tulip tree The tulip tree, also called *yellow poplar,* is in the *magnolia* family. It is an ancient tree, fossil leaves dating back sixty million years having been found in Greenland and Europe. The leaves are squared-off at the ends and deeply notched. Its yellow-green flowers resemble tulips.

F. A. Blashfield; American Forest Products Industries, Inc.

The tulip tree, with its large flowers, pointed leaves, and cone-shaped fruits, is an unusual and beautiful ornamental tree

The wood of the tulip tree is soft and can be easily milled or worked. Enormous amounts are used for plywood, boxes, crates, insulation material, and paper for books. A heart stimulant is derived from its bitter inner bark.

The tulip tree grows in the eastern states west to Wisconsin and south to Louisiana and Florida. D. C. H.

Tumblebug see Scarabs

Tumbleweed Tumbleweed is a name given to at least two plants commonly found in the midwestern and western prairies, plains and deserts. These plants may grow to be two feet tall. When the plants are dead and dry in the autumn, they snap off easily near the ground. Since their foliage is round at the top, the plants are easily blown or tumbled about.

Tumbleweeds sometimes collect in masses and resemble great loosely constructed balls of grass blowing along. They are easily caught in fences or along buildings and may be a nuisance. Plants called tumbleweeds include the *Russian thistle* and one of the *amaranths*. D. J. I.

Tumbleweed, of the amaranth family

Tumor (TWO-mer) A tumor is a growth on or in the body that is not normal. A tumor may occur in any tissue or in any organ of the body.

Some tumors are cancerous, or *malignant*. These grow rapidly with abnormal cell division. Small pieces or groups of cells may break off the original tumor, and be carried by the blood stream to other places in the body, where they grow into new tumors (*metastases*). Malignant tumors are treated by X-rays, surgery, or chemicals.

Other tumors do not spread, but stay in the place where they first started growing. These are called *benign* tumors. If these grow to a large size, they crowd other organs and may be painful if they press upon nerves. They are usually removed by surgery. Moles and warts are benign tumors.

Tumors come from a change in the normal growth pattern of body cells. From birth to adulthood bodily growth goes on at a rapid rate. After a person becomes an adult, growth slows down and is confined to replacement of worn-out cells or to repair of damage done by injury. What causes growth to begin after an injury, or what causes it to stop after the repair has been made, is not known. If something goes wrong with the controls, whatever they are, the growth continues past the point of repair.

It seems to be fairly certain that continual irritation, mechanical or chemical, can result in malignant tumors in persons susceptible to them. J. C. K.
SEE ALSO: CANCER

Tuna The tuna is a well-known food and game fish. Tuna are found in the Mediterranean Sea, and in the Atlantic and Pacific oceans. Tuna fish have bodies shaped like a torpedo with a crescent-shaped tail. They are dark

Bluefin tuna is the largest of the bony fish
Chicago Natural History Museum

blue above and silvery underneath. Full-grown tuna weigh several hundred pounds. Tuna canning is an important industry in the United States, Japan, and Mediterranean and Latin-American countries.

Tuna fishing is done in large boats that travel thousands of miles to look for schools of tuna. When the tuna are sighted, live bait is thrown overboard. The fish swim close to the boat and then are caught.

Tuna are stored in the refrigerated hold of the ship. At the cannery, they are cleaned and precooked.   M. R. L.

Courtesy Society For Visual Education, Inc.

In the northernmost regions of the tundra, the ground remains frozen most of the year

Tundra (TUHN-druh) Tundra is the name given to the land between the forest regions and the areas of permanent snow. The largest tundra on Earth is the vast area of northern Siberia in the Soviet Union. Few people live there. Animals which inhabit the region include musk ox, caribou or reindeer, Arctic hare, lemming and fox. The summer is very short, lasting only about two months.

The word "tundra" is a Russian word meaning *marshy plain*. Such Arctic areas are level and treeless, and remain as perpetual bogs, or marshes. The soil under the surface is always frozen. It prevents the melted surface ice from seeping into the ground. The vegetation which can grow consists mostly of lichens, mosses, and heather.

Tundra is also the name given to the vegetation that is typical of the region.

Geographers often divide tundra into three transitional, vegetation zones. The bush tundra is close to the forests. Dwarf trees and shrubs grow on it. The central zone is grass tundra with large flat beds of mosses. The desert tundra is nearest the Arctic ice. Mosses grow only in little spots, gradually getting more and more scarce as one goes north.   J. F. B.

Tungsten (TUHNG-stuhn) Tungsten is a rare, gray-white metal that belongs to the CHROMIUM family of elements. Because it is hard and resists corrosion, it is used in making the finest cutting tools. It is used for filaments in electric light bulbs because it has a high melting point.

Tungsten has symbol W from its old name, *wolfram*. Its atomic number is 74 and its atomic weight is 183.85 (183.86 with oxygen as the standard).

Tungsten is never found alone in nature. It is found in combination with calcium in the mineral *scheelite* and in combination with iron and manganese in the mineral *wolframite*. These minerals are all salts of the oxide of tungsten and when heated with carbon will give metallic tungsten.

China, with its rich supply of the brown-black wolframite, produces the most tungsten. The United States relies upon the gray or yellow mineral scheelite for its source of the metal. Scheelite and wolframite were once thought to be ores of tin, but in 1781 tungsten was recognized as an element.

"Tungsten" means "heavy stone," a term which refers to its high specific gravity of 19.3 grams per cubic centimeter.   J. M. C.
SEE ALSO: ELEMENTS, METAL

Tunicate see Chordata

Tuning fork see Overtones, Sound

Turbellaria see Planaria

Turbine (TER-bihn) A turbine is a machine which changes the energy of a moving liquid, or gas, into a form of energy which will do work. A turbine is usually named according to the force which drives it. Water turbines, steam turbines, and gas turbines are the three main types.

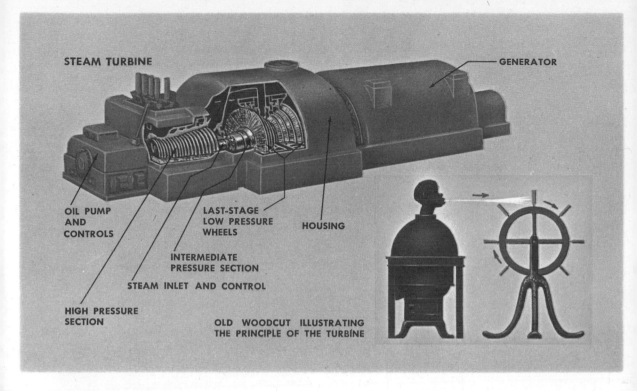

STEAM TURBINE

GENERATOR

OIL PUMP
AND
CONTROLS

LAST-STAGE
LOW PRESSURE
WHEELS

HOUSING

INTERMEDIATE
PRESSURE SECTION

STEAM INLET AND CONTROL

HIGH PRESSURE
SECTION

OLD WOODCUT ILLUSTRATING
THE PRINCIPLE OF THE TURBINE

Water wheels are among the oldest machines man has used to draw energy from nature to do his work. They were turned by a flowing river or stream with a shaft connected to provide simple rotary motion for milling and other uses.

The modern counterpart is the giant hydraulic turbine used at dams and waterfalls to produce electricity. This turbine wheel has many curved blades similar to those of a ship's propeller, and is mounted on a shaft which is connected to generators producing electricity. This turbine wheel is enclosed in a steel case with openings at the top and bottom, and is located at as low a level as possible completely under water beneath a dam or waterfall. The weight and force of a large flow of water rushing down through the turbine causes the blades to spin, turning the generator shaft at high speeds. This turbine, known as a *pressure* or *reaction* turbine, is very efficent.

Another type of water turbine, called a *pressureless* or *impulse* turbine, is used where there is a small amount of water falling from a great height. This wheel has many cup-shaped buckets around the outside diameter. It is driven by water from a nozzle striking the bucket blades, one at a time, at great speeds and force.

The *steam turbine* ranks as one of the most powerful types of machines that man has developed. The steam turbine is made up of a series of wheels which are mounted on a long shaft and increase in size from one end to the other. Each wheel is constructed with many blades, and rotates with the shaft between rows of fixed guide vanes attached to the turbine housing. The steam enters the housing with great pressure, and, directed against the smallest turbine wheel, causes it to rotate as the steam moves on to the next wheel. As the steam moves, its pressure decreases and its volume increases.

The *gas turbine* utilizes a stream of hot gases from a burning fuel to rotate a series of turbine wheels. This type of turbine has a rotating shaft with the turbine wheels at one end and a compressor at the other end. Between is a combustion chamber in which the fuel-air mixture is heated. Air is taken in at the front end of the gas turbine, and compressed into the combustion chamber where fuel is added. As the mixture is ignited, the hot, burning gases rush against the turbine wheels, causing them to rotate; and this, in turn, rotates the compressor. In this manner, heat ENERGY is changed into mechanical energy, and the rotating shaft may be coupled to the workload.   R. J. J.

SEE ALSO: COMPRESSOR, ELECTRICITY, ENGINE, GENERATOR, HYDROELECTRIC POWER, JET PROPULSION, PRESSURE

Turbojet see Engine, Jet propulsion

Turboprop see Jet propulsion

Young tom turkeys being raised on an experimental farm in Kansas

The large leaves and petioles are attached to a short stem. The light-yellow blooms are inflorescences of many small flowers. Processed turmeric is a chemical indicator, used for testing acidity and alkalinity. Its yellow color is used in butter. Its bitter taste is added to curry powder and other products needing some bitterness.　　　　H. J. C.

Turmeric

Turkey Turkeys are the largest game birds and the largest of the domestic FOWL bred for meat. Wild turkeys used to be abundant in North America but are almost extinct. Turkeys had been domesticated in Mexico before the Spanish explorers arrived. Modern turkey breeders have developed smaller turkeys with more breast meat.

Turkeys spend most of their time on the ground. They have heavy bodies and short legs. Domestic turkeys have short wings, but a wild turkey might have a wingspread of almost 40 inches. They have powerful legs, big feet, long necks covered with warty skin, and small, bald heads. The growth of skin that hangs down from the front of the head and laps across the beak is called a *leader* or *dewlap*. The fleshy red lobe on the neck is the *wattle*.

Though some varieties of domestic turkeys are white, most have vari-colored feathers—brown, red, green and black. The feathers shine with a metallic iridescence.

At mating time, the male, or *tom,* struts and gobbles and displays its array of tail feathers spread into a fan.

Turkeys eat seeds, acorns and insects. Young ones are vulnerable to a disease organism that is harbored in damp ground.　C. L. K.

Turmeric (TER-mer-ick) Turmeric is an HERB grown for its useful roots. When dried and powdered, they make a yellow dye and a sharp spice for flavoring. This tropical perennial belongs to the *ginger* family and is native to China, India and the East Indies.

Turnip The part of the turnip plant that is eaten is really both root and stem. Leaves grow from the upper part and roots from the lower. In the first year, the turnip stores up food materials. The next year a yellow flower appears and the plant dies.

This biennial is grown in cool temperate areas and matures in about 70 days. The flavor becomes strong if the weather is too warm. The white to yellow root should be dug up before frost when it is no more than three inches in diameter. Older turnips become woody and are used for animal feed. The tops are used as greens.　　H. J. C.

Turnip

Turpentine Crude turpentine is obtained from a RESIN which a variety of pine trees produce. Crude turpentine is distilled from the resin and a purer product known as *oil of turpentine* is collected. This oil of turpentine is commonly called turpentine.

Turpentine is a colorless liquid which has a characteristic odor. Upon aging and exposure to air, this odor becomes even more pronounced. Since turpentine is an oil, it is insoluble in water; but as other oils, it is soluble in organic solvents such as benzene and ether. In industry, turpentine is used in paints and varnishes to allow them to penetrate wooden surfaces better. Turpentine is a fair solvent for rubber, sulfur, and iodine.

The word "turpentine" is derived from *terpene* which refers to a series of complex HYDROCARBONS. Turpentine is a mixture of some of these terpenes. The chemical formula for turpentine is $C_{10}H_{16}$.   M. S.

Turquoise (TUR-koyz) The best samples of turquoise mineral have a deep, greenish-blue color. It is noncrystalline and has a waxy luster when polished. In America, turquoise was first mined by the Southwest Indians in New Mexico and Arizona. These people still shape and mount them in silver to make prized ornaments.

The word turquoise is from the French word *Turkish* meaning stone. The first gems were brought into Europe by traders who got them in Persia, where they are still mined.

Geologically, turquoise is formed in the earth by deposits from ground-water solutions. It is a hydrous phosphate of copper and aluminum, formula

$$CuAl_6(PO_4)_4(OH)_8 \cdot 4H_2O.$$

It has a hardness of 5 to 6.   D. A. B.

Spiderweb turquoise from New Mexico
J. Daniel Willems

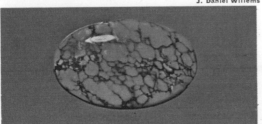

Buchsbaum

The sea turtle's legs are flippers

Turtle A turtle is a reptile that crawls on short legs. Turtles have an attached shell-like house to cover and protect them. Some turtles live only in water, and others live only on land. Some turtles are capable of living both places.

Turtles, tortoises, and terrapins are all turtles; although the name *tortoise* is usually given to a land turtle. A turtle served as food is often called *terrapin*.

A turtle's shell is formed by the backbone and ribs growing together, then becoming covered with plate-like scales. The top shell, or *carapace,* is arched, making it stronger than a flat surface. The bottom shell, or *plastron,* is flat so that the turtle's legs can reach the ground. Some turtles have leathery shells, or shells that cover part of the body. A frightened turtle pulls its head, legs and tail into its shell where its neck folds up like the letter S.

A painted turtle sun-bathing on a log
Courtesy Society For Visual Education, Inc.

1—Common spotted turtle
2—Giant tortoise
3—South American land turtle
4—Diamondback terrapin
5—Warm water green turtle
6—Common snapping turtle
7—Box turtle
8—Australian snake-necked turtle

Turtles have no teeth, but they have horny beaks that can bite hard. The common snapping turtle of North America may grow to two feet in length. It can snap angrily in all directions, even over its back. A mishandled snapper will take off a finger with one quick chop of its beak.

Turtles hatch from eggs. The female digs a hole with its hind feet in soft dirt or sand, or in a rotting log. It lays the eggs in the hole, covers them with earth, and leaves them for the sun's warmth to hatch. It never sees the baby turtles. When the turtles hatch they crawl toward water for protection from animals, for their shells are still soft. Most types of young turtles eat tadpoles, snails, worms, and insects. Each summer the turtle's shell adds an edge to its carapace plates, marking another year's age. Old turtles may have their plate borders worn away. Some species of turtles live longer than any other backboned animal. Some have lived over one hundred years.

Turtles are coldblooded. They must hibernate in the winter when their blood becomes cold. There have been turtles for 175,000,000 years. Some sea turtles were twelve feet long. The Galapagos turtle of today may weigh five hundred pounds.

The brown and yellow tortoise shell comes from the hawk's-bill turtle. Mud turtles, also known as musk turtles or stinkpots because of their odor, will seize a fisherman's bait. They have a vicious bite. The box turtle, dark brown with yellow spots, is relatively harmless. It destroys garden insects and also likes soft or cooked vegetables.   P. G. B.

SEE ALSO: REPTILIA

Turtledove see Dove

Tusks Tusks are changed, or modified, front teeth. They are found on several kinds of animals, such as the elephant, the walrus, and the hippopotamus. The best IVORY, used for carved ornaments, knife handles, and for some white piano keys, comes from elephant tusks. Eskimos use the ivory of walrus tusks, which is of poorer quality, for harpoon points.

In man, the four front TEETH, upper or lower jaw, are called *incisors*. Elephant tusks are long, thickened upper incisors. They lack the enamel coat of human and some other mammalian teeth. Under the enamel layer, the human tooth is composed of dentine. The elephant tusk is a very hard dentine, commonly called ivory.

Tusks of the wild boar (PIG family), hippopotamus, and walrus are modified canine teeth. These animals use their tusks as weapons. The walrus also uses them to pull itself up onto ice and to get clams and other food from the sea bottom.   B. J. C.

Tweeter see High fidelity

Twilight Twilight is daylight which occurs after sunset or just before dawn. It is caused by the reflection of sunlight from the upper parts of the atmosphere while the sun is as much as 18° below the horizon.

Twilight sleep Twilight sleep is a method of putting people *almost* to sleep by using drugs. It is sometimes used in hospitals to take away pain and memory during operations.

Twins see Multiple births

Twins, the see Gemini

Tympanic membrane see Ear

Tyndall effect (TINN-duhl) When a person looks at the sunlit sky, he sees a blue color. When he looks at some kinds of smoky air under white light, the smoke appears bluish to brownish. The changed color of such lighted objects results from a scattering effect of tiny particles in the air. This is called the Tyndall effect. The same effect makes sunlight appear golden at sunrise and sunset.
SEE: COLLOIDAL SUSPENSION, LIGHT

Type see Printing

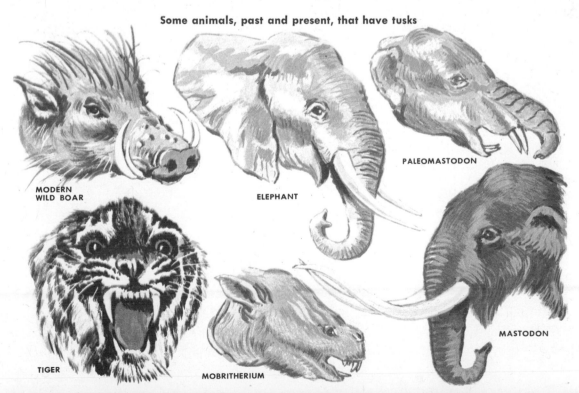

Some animals, past and present, that have tusks

MODERN WILD BOAR

ELEPHANT

PALEOMASTODON

MASTODON

TIGER

MOBRITHERIUM

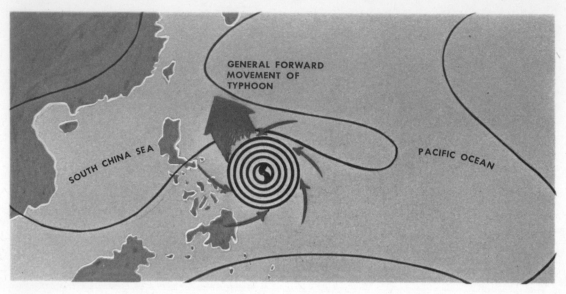

GENERAL FORWARD
MOVEMENT OF
TYPHOON

SOUTH CHINA SEA

PACIFIC OCEAN

Formation and movement of a typhoon in the Pacific Ocean

Typhoid fever (TIE-foyd) Typhoid fever is a disease affecting the intestines. It is spread by foods that contain the germs. In times of disaster, such as flood, fire, and war, sewers frequently break and contaminate a city's drinking water. At such a time typhoid can become an epidemic.

Flies may carry typhoid fever germs on their feet. Some people have recovered from a case of the disease, but are found to harbor the germs in their intestines and can therefore pass them on to others. They are called "typhoid carriers." These carriers are forbidden to work in restaurants or near food.

Symptoms of typhoid are fever; a rose-colored, spot-like rash on the abdomen; bronchitis; and perhaps diarrhea or constipation. Treatment with certain drugs is now effective, and immunization by vaccine serves as a preventative. However, the best precautions are sanitary measures.

Paratyphoid fever is another disease related and similar to typhoid. Typhus fever, however, is a very different disease and not to be confused with typhoid.   J. M. C.
SEE ALSO: DISEASE, TYPHUS FEVER

Typhoon (ty-FOON) Violent tropical storms in the western Pacific Ocean are called typhoons. The same type of storm in the West Indies and Caribbean Sea is called a hurricane. Winds of 75 miles per hour or more occur in these storms.

Typhoons form over tropical oceans when the air is heated and pushed upward. As the air goes up, a huge whirl develops. This circular motion may be several hundred miles in diameter. It continues because heat and water vapor supply the energy.

Typhoons move with the general atmospheric currents, and they travel vast distances. They often cause great damage to coasts, shipping, and islands that lie in their paths. High tides and flooding accompany the devastating winds.   D. E. Z.
SEE ALSO: HURRICANE

Typhus fever (TYE-fuhs) Typhus fever is a disease carried by lice and fleas. It occurs where people are crowded together in poorly-aired, dirty places; where the food is poor; and where lice and rats and fleas live. It has been called "jail fever," "ship fever," and "war camp fever."

The disease is dangerous and highly contagious. Symptoms are complete fatigue, nervous reactions, aching limbs, headache, musty breath, and an eruptive rash the color of dull red mulberries.   J. M. C.

Typography   see Printing

Tyrannosaurus   see Dinosaur

Ulcer An ulcer is an open sore which usually occurs on the skin. Internal sores in the lower part of the esophagus, in the stomach, and in parts of the intestines are also called ulcers.

Sometimes a break in the skin, such as a scratch, becomes infected and forms an ulcer. A special form of TUBERCULOSIS, often a disease of the lungs, may cause ulcers to appear on the skin.

The most common symptom of internal ulcers is pain in the abdomen about three hours after a meal is eaten. Most of the ulcers occurring in the digestive tract are located in the upper small intestine (duodenum). Increased acidity of the digestive juice accompanies such an ulcer. Peptic ulcers are actually caused by the self-digestion of part of the lining of the organ. J. C. K.

Ulna see Skeleton

Ultraviolet ray see Ray, ultraviolet

Umbilical cord see Embryology

Undulant fever see Animal diseases

Ungulata The word *ungulata* means "hoofed." At one time ungulata was the name given to a group of medium and large-sized mammals with hoofed feet. It included such different animals as cattle, deer, hippopotamuses, swine, horses, elephants, and rhinoceroses. Studies show that even though these animals have hoofed feet, they are not close relatives.

Originally hoofed animals may have arisen as a single group from carnivorous stock. As the centuries passed, the animals became so specialized and different from one another that they are no longer put together into one group.

When the first ungulates began to eat grass, they probably had teeth adapted to eating meat. More of them became better adapted for grazing because a gradual series of changes *(mutations)* took place in their teeth. Some of them became abrasive for grinding stems and leaves. This is not true of all present-day plant-eating ungulates. Cows and deer have high narrow teeth, and horses have high broad teeth.

The early ungulates used the whole "hand" and foot for walking. Again, through a series of mutations in some of them, foot structure became changed so that body weight was shifted to the toes. The animals now walked on broadened and hardened toenails or hoofs. Those animals with hoofs could run faster and more easily escape their flesh-eating enemies. Thus more of these survived to reproduce, giving rise, eventually, to many different kinds of ungulates. J. C. K.

Unicellular organism see Protozoa

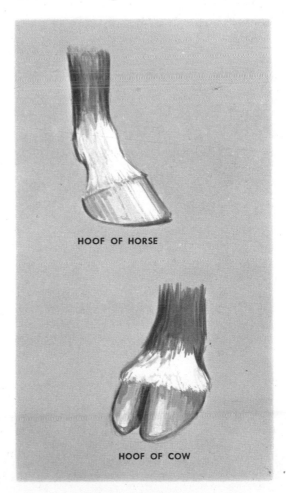

HOOF OF HORSE

HOOF OF COW

Unidentified flying objects Unidentified flying objects (UFO), or flying saucer, are terms used to describe objects thought to have been seen in the sky. No one is yet able to explain them. The most common is the saucer-shaped UFO. There is also the cigar-shaped saucer. Others are shaped like bells.

The written history of the UFO's started over 2000 years ago. As long as history has been recorded, men have spoken of these mysterious objects in the sky.

Reliable sightings were made in France in 1762 by astronomers de Rostan and Croste; in 1831, by Dr. Watermann in Geneva, Switzerland; and in 1849, by Inglis in Gais, Switzerland. The first recorded sighting in the U. S. came in 1882 in Lebanon, Connecticut.

Since then the recorded sightings of UFO's have been few with most of the sources considered unreliable. But in 1947 an American businessman, Kenneth Arnold, sighted a string of UFO's near Mount Rainier. This renewed the public interest in UFO's. In 1948 at Godman Air Base in Madisonville, Kentucky, hundreds saw a strange object in the sky. Captain Mantell piloted a plane and gave chase. He was found dead the next day, his plane having disintegrated before crashing.

Other more recent sightings were made by pilots over Ontario, Canada, in 1952, over Dubuque, Iowa, and Sydney, Australia, in 1960. The pilots gave chase, but no one has yet approached a UFO.

If flying saucers exist, how do they work? Considering their speed and maneuverability, they obviously do not use any of the known methods of flying. Where UFO's come from is not known, but those who believe in them think they come from relatively close distances because of the limitations posed by the speed of light.

Because of the many unreliable reports and the lack of precise research findings, many authorities say UFO's do not exist. Authorities give reasons for the sightings as mirages due to temperature inversions of the atmosphere. Other explanations involve ionization, mist, refraction and reflection, auroras, rainbows, and mock suns. E. Y. K.

Universe The universe includes all the members of the solar system, all the stars in the Milky Way, all of the other stars and galaxies in space, and the space between them. Man does not know where the universe ends—or whether it ends at all. Since ancient times men have been pushing back the boundaries of the known universe. They have wondered, and still wonder, how the universe began and how it will end, when it began, and if it will end.

In ancient times men thought that Earth was the center of the universe. They thought the earth was flat and had a dome fitting down on top of it. The dome was dotted with tiny lights—the STARS. They thought the sun and the stars and the moon were pulled across the dome every day. The Greeks altered this theory. They, too, thought that Earth was the center of the universe, but they imagined that a series of spheres surrounded the earth. These spheres held the sun, the moon, the planets, and the stars. They all revolved around Earth. COPERNICUS and GALILEO introduced, and tried to prove, the theory that the sun, not Earth, was the center of the universe. This idea was difficult for men to accept. Today it is known that neither Earth, nor the sun, nor even the Milky Way galaxy, is the center of the universe. If a person could look at the whole known universe, he would probably notice the MILKY WAY galaxy. But he might not even single out the sun, much less one of the small planets that revolve around it—earth. So far is the earth from being the

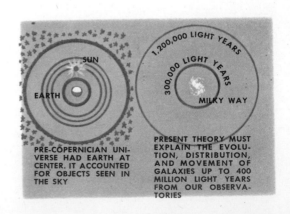

PRE-COPERNICIAN UNIVERSE HAD EARTH AT CENTER. IT ACCOUNTED FOR OBJECTS SEEN IN THE SKY

PRESENT THEORY MUST EXPLAIN THE EVOLUTION, DISTRIBUTION, AND MOVEMENT OF GALAXIES UP TO 400 MILLION LIGHT YEARS FROM OUR OBSERVATORIES

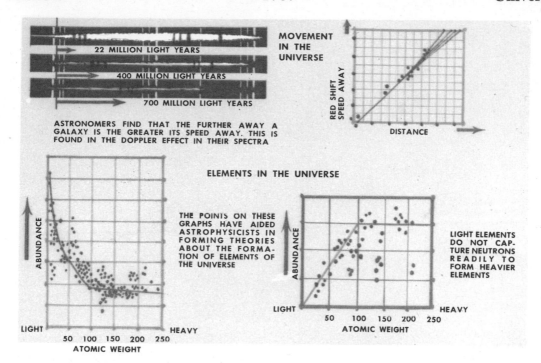

center of the universe that, compared to the entire known universe, Earth would be less significant than a guppy swimming in the Pacific Ocean.

Many people might like to think that the universe has always been just as it is today and that it will always remain the same. But astronomers know that the universe changes. Stars die out. New stars are formed. Stars move in space. Galaxies move. Astronomers use the information they have about the known objects in space—their composition, their directions and speeds, their changes in appearance—to theorize about the origin, evolution, and future of all the rest of the universe.

Most astronomers today agree that observations of distant galaxies indicate that the entire universe is steadily expanding. Since all the galaxies are moving away from each other, astrophysicists sometimes imagine that the universe is an enormous sphere that is expanding like a soap bubble or a balloon that is being blown up.

The recent advancements in the science of NUCLEAR SCIENCE enable astronomers to present new theories about the origin of the universe. The study of nuclear reactions leads to the study of chemical elements, how they are formed, and why they occur in the proportions that they do. When astronomers put such data together with data collected by astrophysicists, they can piece together a little more of the puzzle. The astrophysicists can study what elements are in outer space and in what proportions they occur there. They know that there is a predominance of hydrogen in stars and space. There is also a large amount of helium. Hydrogen and helium are the simplest and lightest elements. High temperature and high pressure are necessary to start the nuclear reactions to form elements.

Some astrophysicists theorize that about 13 million years ago, all the matter in the universe was packed into a tight, small ball— a *primeval nucleus*. This nucleus exploded and began to expand. In the early stages of expansion, the stars and the galaxies were formed. As the universe continues to expand, the galaxies will move at increasing speeds and will continue to recede from each other forever. The density of the galaxies in the universe is forever decreasing. In some far distant epoch, the only stars visible from the earth, if it still existed, would be those of man's own galaxy. This theory is one form of the *evolutionary theory* of the universe and is so called because it assumes that the universe began at a finite time. It depends upon Einstein's theory of general RELATIVITY.

Another form of the evolutionary theory also states that after the explosion of the

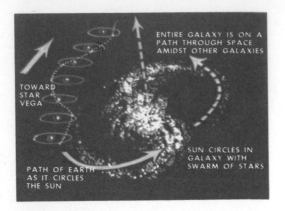

primeval nucleus the stars and galaxies were formed. As the universe expanded, the rate of expansion slowed down. Eventually the forces of mutual gravitational attraction between the galaxies will overcome the expansion. The universe will then start to contract. Eventually all matter will have again contracted into a primeval nucleus. After eons the primeval nucleus will again explode, and expansion will start again. This is the *pulsating model* of the evolutionary theory. Since all matter would be destroyed in this contraction and expansion, astronomers can, of course, have no direct way of determining whether this is a true model.

The *steady-state* theory states that the universe had no beginning and will have no end. Instead of an explosion of a primeval nucleus in the far, far distant past, astronomers who support the steady-state theory claim that matter is being created all the time, at an exceedingly slow rate, in the space between the galaxies. This new matter is hydrogen, and it will eventually form clusters of galaxies. Each new cluster forms, expands, ages, and dies, but other new clusters are always forming so the universe will always have the same density and there will always be galaxies of all ages in the universe. Thus the universe is always the same in any epoch. A major trouble with the steady-state theory is that it violates the laws of THERMODYNAMICS.

The evolutionary theory, on the other hand, states that all galaxies are the same age. The difference in age is apparent, since the light from the most distant galaxies left them many billions of years ago when they were younger.   C. L. K.

SEE ALSO: SPACE, SUN

Ural Mountains see Asia

Uranium (yoo-RAY-nee-um) In 1896 a French chemist, Henri Becquerel, happened to put a piece of mineral containing uranium near a covered photographic plate. He was surprised when he found that the plate was fogged as if it had been exposed to light. After experimenting, he found that some kind of invisible ray came from the uranium. This phenomenon is known today as *radioactivity*.

The mineral Becquerel put near the plate was PITCHBLENDE. In 1898, PIERRE AND MARIE CURIE tried to isolate the radioactive material from a ton of pitchblende. They discovered that pitchblende itself was more radioactive than pure uranium. The first radioactive substance they isolated from pitchblende was called *polonium,* named after Madame Curie's native country, Poland. Later she isolated a small amount of RADIUM. Experiments conducted later by other scientists led to the discovery of other radioactive elements.

Uranium is found chiefly in pitchblende, 80 per cent of which is in the form of an oxide, U_3O_8. *Carnotite* also contains uranium, VANADIUM, and POTASSIUM.

Although uranium is considered a rare element, it is found in moderate quantities in Canada, Republic of the Congo, Czechoslovakia, Colorado, and Utah. Uranium is a metal that is silvery, about as dense as

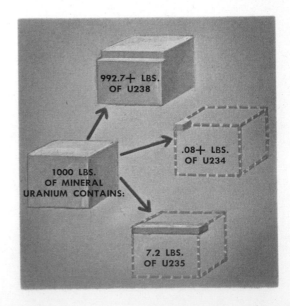

tungsten, slightly softer than steel, and is the heaviest element that occurs in any abundance. Its atomic number is 92, and its atomic weight is 238.03 (238.07, O = 16). It has several isotopes, some of which are important as sources of nuclear energy.

Uranium, like all other radioactive substances, goes through radioactive disintegration, emitting three different kinds of radiations—alpha, α; beta, β; and gamma, γ rays. The half-life of U^{238} is 4.5 x 10^9, or 4½ billion years.   E. Y. K.

SEE ALSO: ELEMENTS, NUCLEAR ENERGY, NUCLEAR SCIENCE

Uranus (YOOR-uh-nuhs) Uranus is one of the giant planets that revolve around the sun. It is the seventh planet away from the sun. Its path is between the paths of SATURN and NEPTUNE. Uranus and Neptune look very much alike because both are about the same size, and have a greenish color. These two planets are sometimes called "twins."

Uranus speeds up in its journey around the sun when it approaches Neptune. After it passes Neptune, Uranus slows down. Neptune's gravity causes the changes in Uranus' speed. From studying these changes in the speed of Uranus astronomers discovered Neptune. Still the position of Uranus did not fit the tables astronomers had charted for it. Eventually PLUTO, the farthest known planet, was also discovered from the study

The orbit of Uranus compared to that of Earth

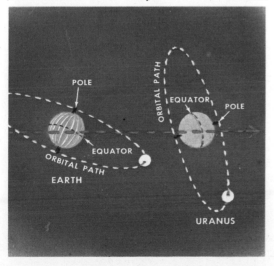

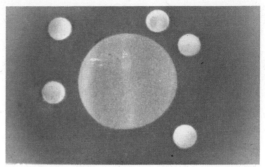

Uranus and its moons

of Uranus' orbit, since Pluto influences Uranus' orbit too.

Uranus was discovered in 1781 by William Herschel, an amateur astronomer. When he first observed this heavenly body, Herschel thought it was a comet. He noticed, though, that its path was circular, like that of a planet. It did not have a tail, as comets do. Thus Herschel decided that it must be a planet.

Uranus can be seen without a telescope, but one needs to know exactly where to look for it. It looks like a very faint star.

With a telescope, Uranus looks like a small green disk. Its greatest difference from the other planets is that it is tilted much more than the others are. Sometimes one of Uranus' poles points almost directly at the earth. Then this planet seems to roll around the sun like a ball instead of spinning around the sun like a top.

Uranus rotates in ten hours and forty-nine minutes, but because of its high angle of inclination (98 degrees), the days and nights —or seasons—are very long. One pole of Uranus sometimes faces the sun for 20 years. Even then, however, Uranus is not warm. Its temperature is less than 300 degrees below zero Fahrenheit. Uranus is too far from the sun to receive much heat or light from it. The sun is about 1,785,000,000 miles from Uranus. Consequently, days on Uranus are cold and dim.

Uranus' orbit is nearly circular. It takes about 84 years for this planet to get around the sun. It travels about 15,000 miles per hour.

Uranus has a diameter of about 30,000 miles. Astronomers differ in their estimates. It is difficult to measure it accurately because of its distance. Even with telescopes, astronomers cannot be too certain about the properties of the distant planets.

Some astronomers think that Uranus has a rock core surrounded by a very thick layer of ice—perhaps six thousand miles thick. Its atmosphere may be three thousand miles deep and may consist mostly of deadly methane gas and frozen ammonia crystals.

Uranus has a system of faint gray belts that run parallel to its equator. The polar regions are slightly flattened, probably because of the rotational speed. Some astronomers have noticed changes in the brightness of Uranus and fuzzy white patches that appear and then go away. These observations could mean that there is some activity on Uranus. Most astronomers do not believe that there could be life similar to ours, however, because of the extreme cold and because of the deadly atmosphere.

Uranus has five moons. Their orbits sometimes seem to be *retrograde,* which means that they seem to go from east to west instead from west to east. The moons' orbits around Uranus' equator, and the changes in the angle of the equator cause the moons to have strange motions when viewed from Earth. When one of the poles points toward Earth, Uranus and its moons give the strange impression of a rolling ferris wheel. When the equator points toward the Earth, it goes from the top to the bottom of the planet instead of from side to side. Then the moons disappear behind Uranus and come up in front of the planet, between Uranus and the Earth. Herschel discovered two of Uranus' satellites. Two more were discovered by another British astronomer, William Lassell. In 1948 in the United States, G. P. Kuiper discovered number five.   C. L. K.

SEE ALSO: NEPTUNE, PLUTO, SATELLITE, SOLAR SYSTEM

Urea (yoo-REE-uh) Urea is the most common single solid material found in human urine. All nitrogen from the breakdown of amino acids from protein, in man and other mammals, is changed to urea and excreted in large amounts in urine. From six to eighteen grams of urea collect in the urinary bladder of man during a 24-hour period.

Rouelle identified urea in 1773. It was the first organic compound ever prepared in a laboratory. This synthesis was accomplished by WOEHLER in 1824. Urea can be broken down to ammonia and carbon dioxide by heat, or by the action of enzymes. The formula of urea is $CO(NH_2)_2$ and the molecular weight is 60.   M. S.

SEE ALSO: ORGANIC COMPOUNDS, PROTEIN

Ureter see Excretory system, Kidney

Urethra see Excretory system, Kidney

Dr. Harold Clayton Urey

Urey, Harold Clayton (1893-   ) Dr. Urey is an American chemist who was awarded the Nobel Prize for Chemistry (1934) for isolating heavy hydrogen. His research helped greatly in the production of uranium for the construction of the atomic bomb.

Harold Urey was born in Walkerton, Indiana, on April 29, 1893. Despite financial difficulties after his father's death, his mother sent him through the county grade schools and high school. After graduation, Urey taught for three years in rural schools. When his family moved to Montana, he followed, and attended the University of Montana.

After receiving his Ph.D. degree at the University of California in 1923, he went to Copenhagen as American-Scandinavian Foundation Fellow to study for a year under the great atomic physicist Niels Bohr.

As an associate professor at Columbia University he performed his first great experiments. In 1931, he discovered heavy hydrogen. He named his discovery *deuterium* from the Greek word meaning second place.

The value of heavy hydrogen to biologists has been enormous. By using it as a tracer element, they can now study proteins, while formerly they had been able to study only simple food-stuffs. They can also explore (with heavy hydrogen) the processes by which living creatures manufacture their own flesh out of the foods they eat.

By 1938 Dr. Urey had isolated heavy hydrogen and certain isotopes of oxygen, nitrogen, and carbon. These elements make up about 96 per cent of all food and flesh. Thus the new isotopes (particularly carbon-14) give research tools to many sciences.

In 1945 Dr. Urey left Columbia and joined the newly-formed Institute for Nuclear Studies at the University of Chicago. Upon retirement from the University of Chicago in 1958, he continued scientific work at the University of California.   D. H. J.

Uric acid (YOOR-ick) Uric acid is a chemical found in the urine of man and other mammals, where it is a breakdown product of PURINES from RNA. In snakes, lizards, and birds, it is excreted in crystals, and some is a product of protein breakdown.

In crystalline form, uric acid is a white, odorless, tasteless solid material. It is slightly soluble in water; but its true acidic nature is evident in its solubility in solutions of alkali hydroxides. It was independently discovered in 1776 by Scheele and by Bergman. Its molecular weight is 168.11; its chemical formula is $C_5H_4N_4O_3$.   M. S.

Urine (YOOR-inn) Urine is an amber-colored liquid excreted by the kidneys. A pigment called *urochrome* gives it its color. The KIDNEYS filter waste materials from the blood. These wastes are passed from the body in the urine. An average adult excretes almost three pints of urine daily.

Urine is somewhat heavier than water. It contains compounds of sodium, chlorine, phosphorus, potassium, calcium, magnesium, and iron. It also contains urea, ammonia, uric acid and creatinine.

The examination of urine is very important in the detection of diseases. G. A. D.
SEE ALSO: EXCRETORY SYSTEM

Ursa Major and Minor

Ursa Major and Minor (ER-suh) Ursa Major and Minor are two groups of stars that are supposed to represent bears in the sky. Ursa Major is the Larger Bear. Ursa Minor is the Smaller Bear. These constellations are probably not as famous as bears as they are for the other figures that some of their stars make—the *Big Dipper* and the *Little Dipper*, which revolve around POLARIS, first one and then the other being upside down.

These constellations can be seen on any clear night in the northern part of the world.

There are several interesting legends about the two star bears. Many early peoples recognized these formations as bears. Each nation made up its own legend. The North American Indians imagined the four bowl stars to be the bear. The three handle stars were hunters who chased the bear. The first hunter carried a bow and arrow. The second carried a pot for cooking the bear. The last one brought the fire. The hunters wounded the bear each autumn, the Indians thought, and as his blood dripped down on the forests it caused the leaves to redden.

In the Greek myths the Greater Bear was the beautiful Callisto, who was changed into a bear by Jupiter to protect her from the jealous Juno. Callisto's son, Arcas, was a hunter. One day he was about to kill the bear that was his mother. Jupiter intervened, changed Arcas into a bear, too.   C. L. K.
SEE ALSO: BIG AND LITTLE DIPPERS, CONSTELLATION

Uterus see Pregnancy

Uvula see Voice

Vaccination see Jenner, Edward; Smallpox; Vaccine

Vaccine (VACK-seen) The term "vaccine" originally referred only to a substance containing the virus of cowpox. In the late 1700's, it was discovered by EDWARD JENNER that persons who had recovered from the disease cowpox could not get the more deadly disease, SMALLPOX. This was a great medical achievement. Jenner scratched the skin of well people and placed material taken from cowpox sores on the open scratch. He found that a man, in whom cowpox had been produced, was then unable to contract smallpox. This resistance against the disease is called *immunity*. *Vaccine* was the name Jenner gave to cowpox matter. The application of vaccine to the open scratch was called *vaccination*.

Today, the word *vaccine* refers to the modified bacteria or virus of any disease which is used to give protection to the person inoculated with it—without producing the severe infection that would result from the untreated virus. Most children in the United States have been immunized against smallpox as well as against diphtheria, tetanus and whooping cough (three in one vaccine). There are now vaccines to prevent many diseases. Some of these are typhoid, typhus and yellow fever. Sometimes the word *vaccination* is used only in reference to smallpox. The application of other vaccines may then be called *inoculation*.

There are three important kinds of vaccine. One is made from a strain of virus or bacteria that has been weakened (*attenuated*). Jenner used this method. The cowpox virus that is scratched into the skin causes a mild disease. As the body fights off this disease, antibodies are formed by the blood. *Antibodies* are protective substances that remain in the blood for a long time. As long as they remain, the person is immune to cowpox and also to deadly smallpox virus, for the antibodies will destroy the germs. This type of vaccine is made from live virus and is sometimes called *live vaccine*. Its protection lasts longer, and the antibodies formed are more numerous, than in other types of vaccines. With many germs, however, it is often difficult to weaken the live germ sufficiently to make its vaccine safe and at the same time to have it effective. Yellow fever vaccine and many veterinary vaccines are of this type. The *Sabin poliomyelitis vaccine* is also a live vaccine. The measles vaccine recently achieved at Harvard University is also an attenuated live vaccine.

A second kind of vaccine is made from dead germs. It can be used only if the germs can be killed and still keep their chemical properties. This kind of vaccine is safe and, like the first type, causes blood to form antibodies. Instead of applying the vaccine to a scratch, it is injected with a hypodermic needle. The disadvantages of this type are that often the antibodies are not as numerous and do not last as long as the antibodies made with live germs. Many vaccines, including the *Salk poliomyelitis vaccine,* are of this killed-vaccine type.

In the third type, antibodies are produced as a result of injecting the treated poisons or

Polio vaccine is produced by growing virus on monkey kidney tissue. The vaccine is stored for two months (left) while it is tested. Three different strains of virus growth are combined for the final vaccine, giving it greater effectiveness

Photos courtesy Chas. Pfizer & Co., Inc.

Special instruments are used to test the strength and purity of growing virus strains

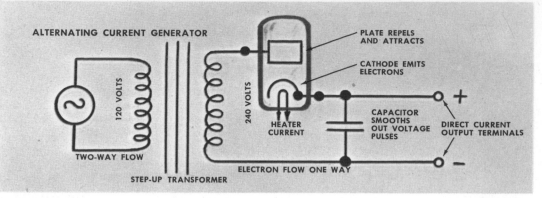

ALTERNATING CURRENT GENERATOR — PLATE REPELS AND ATTRACTS — CATHODE EMITS ELECTRONS — 120 VOLTS — 240 VOLTS — CAPACITOR SMOOTHS OUT VOLTAGE PULSES — DIRECT CURRENT OUTPUT TERMINALS — HEATER CURRENT — TWO-WAY FLOW — STEP-UP TRANSFORMER — ELECTRON FLOW ONE WAY

toxins produced by a germ. Treatment has rendered these toxins harmless. Snakebite, tetanus, scarlet fever and diphtheria are third type vaccines.

Antitoxin is not a true vaccine because it contains antibodies rather than causing them to be produced by the person receiving the antitoxin. Antibodies in antitoxin come from the blood of a horse or cow. The animals either had a disease such as diphtheria or tetanus, and built up antibodies against it, or built them up following the injection of a toxoid. Antitoxins give limited or passive protection while vaccines give active protection. J. C. K.

SEE ALSO: ANTIBODY; BACTERIA, BACTERIOLOGY; DRUGS; MEDICINE; PHARMACOLOGY; SALK, JONAS; VIRUS

Vacuole (VACK-yoo-ohl) A vacuole is a small round transparent-looking particle of fluid found in the cytoplasm of a cell. In protozoans, some vacuoles restore water balance and others digest food.

SEE: PROTOZOA

Vacuum (VACK-yoo-um) A vacuum is generally considered to be a totally empty space. A perfect vacuum is one which contains absolutely no molecules of gas. A perfect vacuum has not been made, though many vacuum tubes are almost free of molecules.

Partial vacuums are obtained in a closed container from which most of the gas molecules have been removed by means of an air pump. A perfect vacuum cannot be obtained because of the mechanical inefficiency of the air pumps. By employing a series of good vacuum pumps, a space can be evacuated to as little as 10^{-8} mm., or .00000001 mm., of mercury as compared to 760 mm. for atmospheric pressure. A. E. L.

Vacuum tube A vacuum tube is the electronic control device used in radio-TV sets, scientific work, and industry. The vacuum tube is so important because it can amplify an electric current; that is, it can produce a strong electric current from a weak one.

Although thousands of different types of tubes are now in use, these are classified by the number of active electrical elements, or electrodes within them. *Diode* tubes, for instance, have two electrodes; *triodes, three; tetrodes,* four; and *pentodes,* five such electrodes. Diodes are used as *rectifiers,* or "electrical one-way streets." The others are used primarily to amplify electrical signals. Vacuum tubes may be seen in actual use when one looks in the back of most radio or TV sets.

As the name implies, all the active parts of the tube are contained within an envelope, a glass or metal tube from which air and other gases have been carefully removed. Each tube contains a CATHODE, a cylinder of nickel alloy coated with the oxides of barium and strontium. When brought to red heat by an internal electric heater, the cathode "boils-offs," or emits, billions of free electrons into the space around it.

In addition, the diode contains a second ELECTRODE, the plate, a cylinder of thin nickel alloy which surrounds the cathode. When the plate of the diode is made positive with respect to the cathode, the plate attracts the negative cathode-emitted electrons strongly, and a current then flows from cathode to the plate. But when the plate is negative, it repels the electrons, preventing their passage and effectively opening the circuit. Thus the diode serves as a rectifier and can convert alternating current into unidirectional current pulses. These may be smoothed by a capacitor into steady direct current.

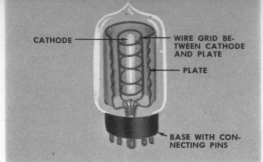

CATHODE

WIRE GRID BE-
TWEEN CATHODE
AND PLATE

PLATE

BASE WITH CON-
NECTING PINS

The triode is made by placing a spiral, or network, of wires between the cathode and the plate. Being closer to the cathode than is the plate, this *grid* can exert a greater influence upon the emitted electrons. Normally the grid is operated at a slightly negative voltage with respect to the cathode, while the plate is made highly positive. The plate thus exerts a strong enough attractive force to overcome the partial repulsive effect of the negative grid.

When an alternating "signal" source is connected in series with the grid circuit, the signal first makes the grid more negative and then less negative. When the signal makes the grid more negative, the grid repels more of the electrons from the cathode and the current reaching the plate decreases. When the signal makes the grid less negative, the grid repels fewer electrons and the plate current increases. Thus a small change of voltage on the grid can cause a large change in the cathode-plate current, and amplification then results.

If sufficient amplification cannot be obtained with one tube, several may be connected in cascade, one after the other. Such an arrangement may increase the effects of a small voltage thousands of times.

If some of the output of an amplifier is fed back in proper phase into its input, or grid circuit, the circuit will act as an oscillator. An OSCILLATOR is an electronic alternating-current generator which generates currents having frequencies in the millions of cycles. Such oscillators are invaluable in radio, TV, long-distance telephony, and industrial processes.

Despite their usefulness, triodes are subject to difficulties due to electrical interaction between the grid and the plate. To eliminate this, a second grid, the *screen grid* is inserted between the first, or *control grid,* and the plate. The screen grid is kept at a potential somewhat less positive than the plate and thus acts as a shield, or screen, between the plate and control grid, preventing interaction between them. The screen-grid also improves the amplification properties of the tube. Such a tube, with a cathode, two grids, and a plate, is a tetrode.

The positive screen grid accelerates (speeds up) electrons traveling from the cathode to the plate. When these electrons reach the plate, they hit it with enough force to knock other electrons off. The secondary electrons knocked off the plate are attracted by the positive screen grid. If enough electrons are attracted to the grid, the plate current will decrease. In a pentode, an additional grid, the *suppressor,* is placed between the screen grid and the plate. The suppressor is usually internally connected to the cathode and is always at cathode potential. The suppressor effectively puts a neutral barrier between the secondary electrons and the screen grid and permits the electrons to return to the plate, thus increasing both stability and the amplification of the circuit.

A beam-power tube is a tetrode (or pentode) specially designed so that the electrons from the cathode travel in sheets between the wires of the screen grid to the plate. Beam-power tubes are frequently used as the final (power) tube in a radio or TV receiver. These tubes have a high power output and high efficiency.

All the tubes just described are primarily receiving tubes. The tubes used in radio, TV, and radar transmitters are similar, but larger so they can handle greater power. At microwave frequencies, special tubes must be used.

Tubes which depend for their operation on the nature of the gas with which they are filled are not, of course, vacuum tubes. Gas-filled tubes such as voltage regulator tubes and thyratrons are finding increasing use, particularly in industrial electronics. The term *electron tube* which covers both gas-filled and evacuated tubes is thus coming into general use, rather than vacuum tube.

Many of the jobs which tubes have done for years can also be done by transistors. For many applications, however, especially where subject to heat or radiation, tubes are still preferable and will be for many years.   C. F. R.

SEE ALSO: ELECTRICITY, ELECTRONICS, PHOTOELECTRICITY, RADIO, TELEVISION, TRANSISTOR

Vagus nerve see Nervous system

Valence (VAY-lens) In chemistry, valence is the ability of an element to combine with another element. Valence of an element is measured by the number of hydrogen atoms it can unite with or, if it will not unite with hydrogen, how many hydrogen atoms it will displace. Many ELEMENTS have more than one valence, and inert gases have zero valence.

Valley A depression or channel cut by a stream or a glacier is called a valley. Valleys are cut deeper by their streams or by ice and snow. The sand and gravel are used as tools to carve or erode the bedrock and remove the loose material. If a stream cuts a valley, the rate of deepening depends upon the speed of the stream, its volume, the kind and amount of sand and rock, and the hardness or resistance of the bedrock.

As running water in any form moves over the surface of the earth, it forms these depressions called valleys. In the beginning, these valleys are usually V-shaped in cross section, although the sides may vary in steepness. Even if a young valley is steep-sided, it does not remain this way. The valley changes over thousands of years and becomes wider and more U-shaped. Valleys go through periods of youth, maturity, and old age. Because a glacier, unlike a river, is in contact with an entire valley floor and a large part of the valley walls, it is able to erode them directly. Glacial valleys are U-shaped up to the point on the valley wall the glacier reached.   V. V. N.

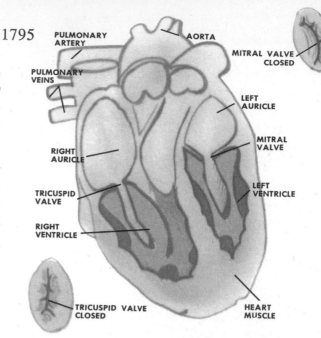

A glacial valley among mountains
Courtesy Society For Visual Education, Inc.

Valves, circulatory Valves are flaps of tissue extending out from the walls of the heart, medium-sized veins, and lymph vessels. They have a door-like action, preventing blood or lymph from flowing backward.

Two important valves in the mammalian HEART are the *mitral* and *tricuspid* valves located between the *auricles* and *ventricles*. In the center of each valve is a cartilage plate, covered on each side by elastic connective tissue containing smooth muscle.

Semilunar valves are crescent-shaped and found in the heart openings to the *pulmonary artery* and *aorta*. They are similar to the mitral and tricuspid valves.

Valves are commonly found in the veins coming back to the heart from the arms and legs. Usually they occur just before the junction or union of two branches. The free edges of the crescent-shaped valves face in the direction of the flow of blood. Beneath their covering of *endothelium,* in the cup part of the crescent, is elastic connective tissue. The CONNECTIVE TISSUE continues into the elastic membrane of the vein (*tunica intima*).

The construction of the valves in the lymph vessels is almost identical to those in the veins.   J. C. K.

SEE ALSO: CIRCULATORY SYSTEM

Vampire see Bat

Van Allen belts see Atmosphere

Van de Graaff see Accelerator

Vanadium (vah-NAY-dee-uhm) Vanadium is element number 23. It is a metal, used in steel. Vanadium alloys are hard and malleable. It is found in several ores. It was first identified in 1830 by Nils Sefstrom, a Swedish chemist. It has chemical symbol V. Its atomic weight is 50.942 or 50.95 with oxygen as the standard.

It is very difficult to obtain pure vanadium because reduction from the ore requires very high temperatures. Also, pure vanadium reoxidizes very easily. Vanadium pentoxide (V_2O_5), one of the most widely used compounds, is used in the oxidation of napthalene and the manufacture of sulfuric acid. Other compounds are used in inks, paints and varnishes, insecticides, glass, etc.   M. S.
SEE ALSO: ELEMENTS

Vane see Wind vane

Vanilla (vuh-NILL-uh) Vanilla is a vine related to the ORCHID. Man takes (extracts) a flavoring from it that is also called *vanilla*. The plant is tropical and has been cultivated in Mexico for a long time. It is grown widely in Madagascar and the Comoro and Reunion islands. A synthetic vanilla is often used today.

The vanilla plant is a climbing orchid

The vanilla vines climb by means of air rootlets which twine about trees. They live for ten years or more. A plant produces pods, or beans, five to ten inches long, which resemble large green beans. They are picked when a yellow green color, and allowed to dry and "cure." The inside pulp is an oily mass which contains small seeds. The beans are cut up, and by a complex process the vanilla flavoring is extracted from the pulp. Because the cost of production is high, substitutes (such as tonka beans) have been developed which are very good, although none quite achieve the quality of the true vanilla.   D. J. I.

Vapor A vapor is the GAS form of a material which is usually a liquid. When water, for example, is heated, it becomes a vapor. The molecules of a vapor behave like those of an ordinary gas.
SEE: HUMIDITY, PRECIPITATION

Vapor lamp see Bulb, electric

Vapor pressure see Boyle's Law, Charles' Law, Gas

Vaporization see Evaporation, Heat of vaporization

Variable star see Star, variable

Varicose veins (VAIR-uh-kohss) Varicose VEINS is a disorder in which veins near the surface of the skin become enlarged and knotty. When blood returning to the heart slows down because the valves in the veins fail to work properly, blood backs up in the veins and hard, knotty swellings, generally dark-blue in color, appear. They may burst, causing dangerous bleeding. Varicose veins are most common in the legs, but may occur elsewhere.

Varnish Varnish is a clear coating to be sprayed or spread on a surface. It is made by dissolving resins in alcohol or volatile oils. A volatile oil is one from which vapor will escape rapidly, or dry quickly. It is made from a vegetable source.

Varnish made with alcohol as a drying agent is called *spirit varnish*. That made with volatile oil is an oil varnish. The resins used are secured from various trees; copal from Africa and lac, from which shellac is made, from Asia. No pigments (color) are added to varnish, as the chief use of varnish is to bring out the natural grain of wood and give it a protective finish.

Lacquer is somewhat similar in its content and drying qualities, and PIGMENT is added for color. A lacquer finish on wood gives a very smooth finish and is much thinner and harder than any paint coat. However, a lacquer coat is affected by steam heat and humidity, and will crack and chip from the wood. Lacquer is also used on metal when a delicate shading of color is needed in design. P. G. B.

Vascular bundle (VASS-kyuh-ler)

Higher plants develop cells which form in groups during the first year of growth. These are called vascular bundles. They carry materials up and down the plant.

Vascular bundles have three kinds of tissues. *Xylem* conducts water and raw materials up the plant. *Phloem* carries food down to the roots. In woody plants, these two groups of cells are separated from each other by the vascular *cambium*. The cambium cells divide again and again, making more cells.

The vascular tissue produced after the first year, as in biennials and perennials, forms concentric circles rather than bundles. These are the ANNUAL RINGS. The primary xylem and phloem, or vascular bundle, gets pushed to the outside as new tissue is produced by the cambium. H. J. C.

SEE ALSO: PLANT TISSUES

The structure of vascular bundles (in monocot and dicot plants)

Courtesy Society For Visual Education, Inc.

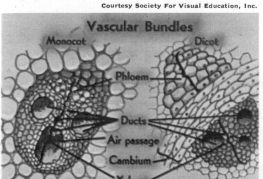

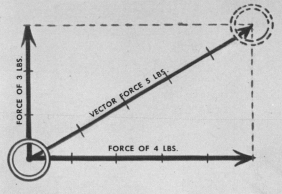

IF A FREE PARTICLE IS PUSHED UPWARD BY A FORCE OF 3 LBS. AT THE SAME TIME IT IS PUSHED RIGHT WITH A FORCE OF 4 LBS., THE VECTOR ANSWER FOR THE RESULT OF THESE TWO (VECTOR) FORCES IS SHOWN BY THE DIAGONAL VECTOR, 5 LBS.

Vector (VEHK-tehr) When a quantity has both direction and magnitude (size), it is called a *vector* quantity. If the quantity has only magnitude, it is called a *scalar* quantity.

Such measurements as volume mass, time, and temperature are usually thought of as merely numbers indicating a certain amount of each. These are some *scalar* quantities. On the other hand, when one thinks of displacement, velocity, and ACCELERATION, the idea of direction, as well as amount, comes to mind.

When the magnitude of the vector quantity is considered without regard for its direction, it becomes a scalar quantity. For instance, if one is interested only in the rate at which an automobile can travel regardless of direction, the VELOCITY becomes a scalar quantity designated as speed. Similarly, length may be the scalar quantity of the vector displacement.

In a diagram, a vector quantity is generally indicated by drawing an arrow pointed in the proper direction. The point of the arrow is called the *terminus,* and the butt end of the arrow is called the *origin*. In mathematical expressions, a vector quantity is designated by drawing a small arrow above the letter used to represent the quantity, such as A or B, or, more often, the A or B symbols will be printed in bold-face type, such as **A**. A. E. L.

ALFRED B. NOBEL
1833–1896 •
Invented dynamite,
started Nobel Prizes

HIPPOCRATES
460–370? B.C •
"Father of Medicine"

MARIE CURIE
• 1867–1934
Discovered radium
and polonium

ENRICO FERMI
• 1901–1954
Produced first atomic pile and first
controlled nuclear chain reaction

THOMAS ALVA EDISON
1847–1931 •
Invented light bulb,
phonograph and mimeograph

NICOLAUS COPERNICUS
• 1473–1543
First astronomer to say that Earth
goes around the sun

LUTHER BURBANK
• 1849–1926
Invented new
varieties of plants

EDWARD JENNER
1749–1823 •
Discovered smallpox vaccine

CHARLES DARWIN
1809–1882 •
Conceived the Theory of Evolution
through Natural Selection

WILLIAM HARVEY
• 1578–1657
Discovered the circulation
of the blood

GEORGE WASHINGTON CARVER
1864–1943 •
Experimented with
practical botany

SAMUEL F. B. MORSE
• 1791–1872
Invented telegraph and Morse code

LOUIS PASTEUR
• 1822–1895
Invented pasteurization

BENJAMIN FRANKLIN
• 1706–1790
Invented lightning rod